G[ ]
H[ ]
TRANSPORT
by Road *&* Air

Guidelines for HORSE TRANSPORT by Road & Air

Edited by Catherine W. Kohn

Copyright © 2000 by American Horse Shows Association, Nevins Farm & Equine Centre of The Massachusetts Society for Prevention of Cruelty to Animals.
All rights reserved under the Pan-American and International Copyright Conventions.
American Horse Shows Association, Inc.
220 East 42nd Street, New York, NY 10017
Phone: 212-972-2472
Fax: 212-983-7286
This book may not be reproduced in whole or in part in any form or by any means, electronic or mechanical, including photocopying, recording, or by any information storage and retrieval system now known or hereafter invented, without written permission from the publisher, American Horse Shows Association.
MADE COMPLETELY IN THE U.S.A.
1st printing: March 2000
Library of Congress Catalog Number: 00-132617
ISBN: 0-9700169-1-3

TABLE OF CONTENTS

- **INTRODUCTION** 9
  By Catherine W. Kohn, VMD, Diplomate ACVIM

- **GUIDELINES FOR TRANSPORT** 19
  By Catherine W. Kohn, VMD, Diplomate ACVIM

- **STUDIES OF THE CAUSES OF TRANSPORT-ASSOCIATED STRESS AND SHIPPING FEVER IN ATHLETIC HORSES** 35
  By Masa-aki Oikawa, DVM, PhD & James H. Jones, DVM, PhD

- **ENVIRONMENTAL, HEMATOLOGICAL AND BLOOD BIOCHEMICAL CHANGES IN EQUINE TRANSIT STRESS** 63
  By D.P. Leadon, MA, MVB, MSc, FRCVS; J. Daykin, BVSc, MRCVS; W. Backhouse, BVSc, MRCVS; C. Frank, MRCVS; & M. A. Atock, MRCVS

- **BODY WEIGHT, RECTAL TEMPERATURE, HAEMATOLOGY AND BLOOD CHEMISTRY PRIOR TO TRANSPORT AND FOR THREE DAYS AFTER ARRIVAL IN RACEHORSES TRANSPORTED BY AIR TO INTERNATIONAL RACES IN HONG KONG** 71
  By D.P. Leadon, MA, MVB, MSc, FRCVS & K. Watkins, BVSc, MRCVS

- **EFFECTS OF TRANSIT ON THE RESPIRATORY SYSTEM OF THE HORSE** 83
  By N. Edward Robinson, BVetMed, MRCVS, PhD

- **EFFECTS OF TRANSIT ON THE IMMUNE SYSTEM OF THE HORSE** 93
  By Melissa T. Hines, DVM, PhD, Diplomate ACVIM

- **DOES TRANSPORT STRESS AFFECT EXERCISE PERFORMANCE IN HORSES** 103
  By L. Jill McCutcheon, DVM, PhD & Raymond J. Geor, BVSc, MVSc, Diplomate ACVIM.

- **BIBLIOGRAPHY** 117

INTRODUCTION

by Catherine W. Kohn, VMD, Diplomate ACVIM

Horses of all types are required to travel to take part in the diverse activities of equestrian sport and competition. For some horses, travel times and distances may be short, whereas others may spend several consecutive days in a road transport vehicle or may fly for many hours to compete. For humans, prolonged travel is stressful and fatiguing. Despite a large body of research on the effects of transport on humans and horses, there is a surprising lack of specific information on the effects of transport on the health and performance capacity of human or equine athletes.

The choice of Sydney, Australia for the 2000 Olympic Games has focused the attention of the equine industry on the effects of transport on horse health and performance. To address these issues, an *International Workshop on Equine Transport,* sponsored by the Nevins Farm and Equine Centre of the Massachusetts Society for the Prevention of Cruelty to Animals, was held March 11-14, 1999, in Middleburg, Virginia. Participants in the Workshop were:

- Dr. Catherine W. Kohn — Department of Veterinary Clinical Sciences, The Ohio State University, Columbus, OH, Co-chairperson

- Professor Leo B. Jeffcott — Dean and Professor of Veterinary Clinical Studies, University of Cambridge, Cambridge, United Kingdom, Co-chairperson

- Dr. A. Kent Allen — Virginia Equine Imaging, Middleburg, VA, Co-chairperson

- Dr. Ray Geor — Kentucky Equine Research, Versailles, KY

- Dr. Melissa T. Hines — Department of Veterinary Clinical Medicine and Surgery, Washington State University, Pullman, WA

- Dr. James H. Jones — Department of Veterinary Surgical and Radiological Sciences, University of California, Davis, CA

- Dr. Desmond Leadon — Irish Equine Centre, Naas, Ireland

- Dr. Jill McCutcheon — Department of Veterinary Pathobiology, University of Guelph, Ontario, Canada

- Dr. Masa-aki Oikawa — Vice Director Equine Research Institute, Japan Racing Association, Utsunomiya, Japan

- Dr. N. Edward Robinson — Department of Large Animal Clinical Sciences, Michigan State University, East Lansing, MI

- Mr. Joe Silva — Nevins Farm and Equine Centre, Massachusettes Society for the Prevention of Cruelty to Animals, Boston, MA

- Dr. Frits Sluyter — Federation Equestre Internationale, Lausanne, Switzerland

- Dr. Nathaniel White — DuPont Equine Medical Center, Virginia Polytechnical Institute, Leesburg, VA

- Mr. James R. Wolf — United States Equestrian Team, Gladstone, NJ

The purposes of the Workshop were to discuss all published information on transport of horses, to identify transport-related risk factors for disease and poor performance, and to generate guidelines for safe transport. Five state-of-the-art review papers on transport of horses were authored by Workshop participants and are included for reference in this publication. References to these review papers appear in parenthesis (authors' names only) in the Introduction and Guidelines chapters. In addition, the Workshop participants identified the most important unanswered questions about transport in horses, and formulated a group of related research hypotheses designed to answer these questions and collectively to significantly advance our understanding of risk factors in transport. Funding for these projects is currently being sought. There is a plan to convene the Workshop regularly to review progress, redirect research efforts, and update the Guidelines for Transport.

RISK FACTORS FOR HORSES DURING TRANSPORT

■ Stress

Stress has been defined as ".. a complex mosaic of responses by which an animal attempts to maintain homeostasis in the face of environmental challenges" (Oikawa and Jones). Although transport is in general thought to be stressful for horses, there are large individual variations in responses. Some horses appear to adapt well to transport, while others do not and may be more likely to experience transport-related diseases such as shipping fever and colic. There is no direct evidence to date that the stress of transport results in immunosuppression in horses; however, studies of the responses of the equine immune system to transport are limited. More data and better methodology are required to assess the immunocompetence of transported horses (Hines).

■ Effects of transport environment on the respiratory system

Horsemen have long been aware that some animals become ill during or following transport. The most common illness is respiratory infection, so called shipping fever or transport-related respiratory disease. Horses become depressed, febrile, and inappetant. Increased respiratory rate, nasal discharge, and cough may also be noted. Signs may develop during shipping or up to 3 days following arrival at the destination. Leadon (1990) estimates that 30 to 40% of horses that develop shipping fever after air transport are afebrile until 2 to 3 days after transport. Of racehorses transported 25-28 hours by road in Japan, 11.9% developed shipping fever and the incidence of disease increased as the travel time increased (Oikawa and Jones). Three of 8 (37%) Thoroughbred racehorses transported 41 hours by road had shipping fever after 20 hours of transport (Oikawa and Jones). Leadon reported that 7 of 112 (6.3%) of horses shipped by air in open stalls from the UK to Australia developed shipping fever within 2 days of arrival. Percentages of horses affected during air travel are likely significantly increased now because of the use of enclosed air-stables (containers) (Figure 1) on pallets (Leadon). Horses transported by road or air may exhibit some or all of these clinical signs and, in severe cases, disease may progress to life-threatening pneumonia/pleuritis.

Why is transport associated with respiratory disease? Although the answers to this question must be clarified by research, there are several hypotheses, relating to the transport environment and to the ability of the horse's respiratory system to respond to the challenges of the transport environment. Concentrations of airborne contaminants are

Figure 1: *A horse loaded in an air-stable during transport to the airplane. Photograph courtesy of Dr. Mark Ravenaugh.*

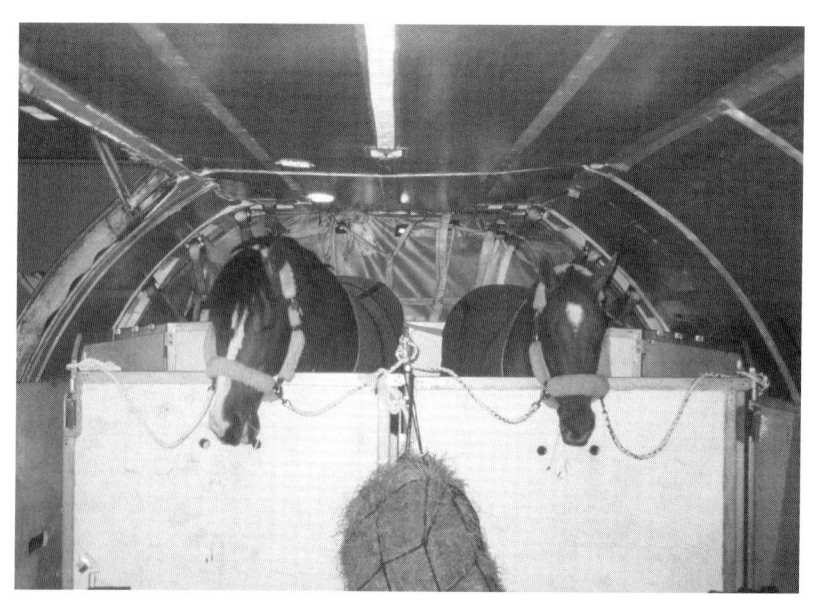

Figure 2: *Horses confined in open stalls on an airplane. Note hay in the horses' breathing zone. Photograph courtesy of Dr. Mark Ravenaugh.*

increased in road transport vehicles and in planes. Bacterial concentrations in the air in planes have been shown to increase as the length of the flight increases. Bacterial concentrations in air are particularly high when a plane remains on the ground for any period, especially if auxiliary ventilation systems are not employed (Leadon). Other respirable particles in the air include organic dusts from hay and bedding that may contain mold spores. The same is likely to be the case in road transport vehicles. Dust concentrations in horse trailers are reported to be higher than concentrations known to be hazardous to humans (Robinson). Concentrations of airborne contaminants in the horse's breathing zone, the source of inspired air, are particularly important. Horses shipped with hay nets close to their noses and with deep bedding are likely to have an especially high particulate content in breathing zone air (Figure 2).

Healthy horses defend themselves from inspired particulate matter by regularly clearing their airways of mucous secretions (that may increase as a result of airway irritation) and inspired particles. Efficient removal of mucus and debris requires a head down posture to facilitate clearance of the airways by the mucocilliary system (*i.e.*, cells that propel secretions toward the nose and mouth for removal by cough and expectoration). For safety during transport, horses are confined and restrained in a head up position. In experiments on the effects of the head up position on airway clearance, it has been shown that bacterial counts increase in tracheal fluid within 6 to 12 hours of restraint. When horses were allowed to lower their heads at will, bacterial counts in tracheal fluids decreased within 12 hours. Allowing horses to lower their heads for 30 minutes every 6 hours did not prevent the increase in tracheal fluid bacterial concentrations (Robinson). Although the effects of the head up posture during transport have not yet been studied, we suspect that the head up posture may be an important risk factor for development of shipping fever.

Without sufficient air changes, ambient temperature and humidity increase in transport vehicles in proportion to the stocking density of horses. Temperature and humidity in aircraft will also vary based on time in flight and positions of horses in the aircraft. Leadon demonstrated that the temperature in airplanes decreased from $20.7 \pm 3.4°C$ to $17.9 \pm 2.7°C$, and that the relative humidity decreased from $71 \pm 9.1\%$ to $37.8 \pm 0.6\%$ during flight. There was a gradient in temperature and relative humidity from front to rear of the plane, both when stationary and in flight, with the rear of the plane being significantly warmer and more humid. Similar studies have not yet been performed in road transport vehicles; however, increased ambient temperatures in stationary vehicles are a common problem for horses transported by road in hot weather. Appropriate equine thermoregulatory responses to heat include increased respiratory rate and sweating. Elevations in respiratory rate and/or effort (taking deeper breaths) may also facilitate increased delivery of respirable particles such as bacteria to the lung. Dehydration can develp during long distance transport, either as a result of decreased water intake and/or sweat fluid losses during hot weather transport. Importantly, sweat fluid losses can also be substantial in cooler weather when ventilation in the transport vehicle is inadequate and horses are excessively blanketed. Such fluid losses may alter the character of tracheal mucus, increasing its viscosity, and making the mucus, and associated contaminants, more difficult to clear from the airways.

Studies of horses with shipping fever during or following long distance road transport in Japan have shown that the most common bacterial agent isolated from affected horses is *Streptococcus equi var zooepidemicus*. This organism is a common commensal inhabitant of the nasopharynx and guttural pouches of horses (Oikawa and Joncs). These investigators hypothesize that when normal mucosal defense mechanisms are compromised during transport, *S zooepidemicus* organisms invade the lower airway causing shipping fever. In addition, horses with preexisting (pretravel) subclinical respiratory disease probably have an even greater risk of developing shipping fever during transport.

Why do some horses develop shipping fever while others, exposed to the same environment, do not? The reasons for the greater susceptibility of some horses to transport-associated respiratory disease are unclear. It is possible that horses that become ill are particularly compromised by the effects of the enforced head up posture on airway clearance mechanisms. Accumulation of airway secretions and debris in these horses may be a result of a particularly large ventilatory response (*i.e.* faster respiratory rate and/or increased minute ventilation [volume of air inspired per minute]) and delivery of many bacteria and other respirable particles to the lung. Horses with a less profound ventilatory response may be the ones that do not become ill during transport.

■ Effects of transport on the gastrointestinal system

Prolonged confinement in a transport vehicle in association with reduced feed intake and altered eating patterns may depress gastrointestinal motility. Gut stasis may predispose the horse to colic or enterocolitis and diarrhea. The incidence of gastric ulceration during transport is unknown and is the subject of current research. Horses that develop gastric ulceration when confined to a stall may have a similar response during long journeys. Gastric ulceration may cause depression, colic, and inappetance. Signs may persist for days to weeks following transport if appropriate antiucler therapy is not administered.

■ Negative energy and fluid balance during transport

Horses lose weight during transport by road or air at a rate of approximately 0.45 to 0.55% body weight/hour (Mars *et al* 1992, van den Berg *et al* 1997) and weight deficits may persist for 3 to 7 days after transport. Weight loss may be partially the result of the "work" required of the horse during transport. Repetitive postural adjustments to the motion of the transport vehicle require continual muscular effort. In one study of ponies transported by road, the energy expenditure of transport was similar to the energy expenditure of walking (Doherty *et al* 1997, Geor). Others have estimated that energy expenditure during travel is twice resting energy expenditure (Oikawa). Prolonged transport, especially by road, may be fatiguing for horses. When the road journey is long, energy expenditure would be significant and muscle glycogen stores may become depleted. In addition, caloric intake is likely decreased during transport. Because of the risk of colic, perhaps due to gut stasis during transport, grain feeding should be reduced; this practice enhances the risk of low caloric intake.

Suboptimal water intake and sweating caused by high temperatures within transport vehicles may result in dehydration. Although fluid deficits may be replaced rapidly (within the first 24 hours) by horses that drink well after transport, complete rehydration may not be achieved immediately. Decreased amounts of large intestinal ingesta and lower ingesta water content in horses that do not drink adequately after transport may reduce the extent of a fluid reservoir that is important for endurance exercise.

■ Duration of travel

As the length of the journey increases, the risk of shipping fever increases. In addition, weight losses are more extensive following transport of longer duration/greater distance. In one study, weight loss (as a percentage of body weight) was 1.1% to 1.6% after 2.5 hours (a 129 km journey) and 3.5% to 5.2% after 60 hours (a 2,921 km journey) (Oikawa and Jones). Dehydration progresses as the duration of travel increases. Because progressive dehydration can occur, it is clear that long road journeys should be punctuated by rest periods and access to water that allow horses to partially recover from the effects of transport that would otherwise be cumulative.

■ Vehicle design and road characteristics
Ventilation in the road transport vehicle or plane is extremely important. Air quality should always be excellent. Because of the high concentration of air contaminants in transport vehicles, ventilation systems that supply suboptimal numbers of air exchanges per hour may increase the risk of respiratory disease in transported horses. Both ground transport vehicles and planes ventilate poorly when stationary. Vehicles designed to utilize high stocking densities are more likely to have inadequate ventilation for transported horses, and may result in greater stress during transport. The stocking density on pallets during air transport is likely to have a significant effect on air quality, temperature and humidity in the plane. The expense of air travel for horses may dictate a higher stocking density (3 or 4 to a pallet) whereas some consigners may prefer to ship their horses 1 or 2 to a pallet. The optimum stocking density has not been identified and is the subject of on-going research.

Road transport vehicles that do not minimize oscillations and vibrations may increase the stress of transport. Leaf spring suspension and low pressure radial tires are reported to provide the smoothest ride (Oikawa and Jones). Rough roads, and routes requiring multiple accelerations and decelerations result in a ride that is more stressful for horses than a ride over smooth roads at a steady pace.

■ Position in the vehicle
Although individual horse preferences vary, as many as 65% of horses, when loose in a road transport vehicle, prefer to ride facing backwards (Oikawa and Jones). Other horses may select a sideways slanted position. Transport in the face forward position may be stressful for many horses.

■ Transmeridian translocation in air travel (Jet lag)
Transmeridian travel may disrupt the circadian rhythms of body temperature, heart rate, cortisol concentrations, and sleep and activity patterns (McCutcheon). In humans, the rate of adjustment of body rhythms after eastward travel is 50% slower than for westward travel, although there is a large individual variation in travelers. After 6 to 8 hours of eastward travel, humans required 8 days to readjust, as compared to 3 days for equivalent westward travel. Evidence of performance impairment has been demonstated in humans for 5 days after 7 hours of eastward travel. However, the effects of jet lag on horses have been infrequently studied, and there are no reports of the effects of jet lag on equine performance (McCutcheon).

■ Effect of Transport on Performance

There are few data on the effect of transport on the performance of equine athletes. It is clear that horses that become ill during transport may perform poorly if not allowed sufficient recovery time before competition, or, if severely ill, may be unable to compete. However, the effect of transport on the performance of horses that remain healthy during transport has been infrequently studied. There was little effect on performance (time trials) of 8 Quarter Horses or Thoroughbreds transported for 8.1 km (15 minutes) or 194 km (2 to 2.5 hours) (Leadon *et al.* 1994). Sprint times and heart and respiratory rates after running of 10 fit Thoroughbred race horses accustomed to transport were not affected by 129 km transport (2.5 hours) (Japanese Equine Research Institute 1997, Oikawa and Jones). These studies suggest that road transport <3 hours has little effect on subsequent athletic performance; however, investigators did not assess the effects of longer journeys or air transport on performance.

It is difficult to study the effects of transport on performance because there are many confounding variables including, for example, athletic ability of each horse, degree of fitness, and food intake during shipping. Although data are lacking, we hypothesize that long road or plane journeys may adversely affect performance. This is another reason that an adequate recovery period should be planned for the end of the journey. Further research is required to clarify the relationships between performance and transport.

GUIDELINES FOR TRANSPORT OF HORSES

by Catherine W. Kohn, VMD, Diplomate ACVIM

These guidelines are based on current information on transport in horses. There are many unresolved issues, and the guidelines will no doubt be modified as the research initiative increases our understanding of the effects of transport on horses. These guidelines build on the previous work of Desmond Leadon MA, MVB, Msc, FRCVS, Charles Frank MRCVS, and Alex Atock MRCVS in *Recommendations to Horse Owners and their Representatives on the Transport of Horses*, published by the Federation Equestre Internationale in July of 1990.

Recommendations are offered as guidelines for transport of all horses whatever the intended post-transport activity or length of the journey. Recommendations for management of horses have been divided into 3 categories: before, during, and after transport. Many of these recommendations apply both to road and air transport; however, comments specific to each mode of transport have also been included. These guidelines represent the collective wisdom to date. As we learn more about transport through our research initiatives, the guidelines will be suitably amended and expanded.

BEFORE TRANSPORT

■ Health status of the horse

Horses that are sick when loaded on the vehicle will be sicker when they get off the vehicle after travelling. It is extremely important to avoid transporting sick horses unless a medical emergency requires transport. Horses with mild or subclinical illness prior to transport are at far greater risk to develop shipping fever. To ensure the health of horses prior to transport, it is wise to monitor rectal temperatures for several days before travel. An adult horse with a temperature of >38.3° C, (101° F) a foal (<6 months of age) with a temperature > 38.9° C (102°C) should not be transported until the cause of the fever has been identified and treated. Horses to be transported should be isolated from horses with respiratory diseases for at least 2 weeks prior to transport. A longer isolation period may be required if exposure to strangles (*Streptococcus equi var equi*) is suspected. Check the vaccination status of horses to be transported. Although there is currently much debate on the efficacy of available vaccines, vaccination at least 2 weeks prior to travel is recommended in North America for adult horses not maintained on a routine vaccination program against Equine Influenza and Equine Herpes Viruses 1 and 4.

Carefully assess your horse's hydration status before long distance transport. Has the horse been drinking sufficient water during the week prior to shipping? If you are concerned, ask your veterinarian to check the horse's capillary refill time, heart rate, and skin tenting. For horses with questionable hydration, ask the veterinarian to evaluate packed cell volume (PCV), total protein (TP), creatinine concentration, and urine specific gravity to more precisely assess the horse's hydration status. Many horses have decreased voluntary water consumption while traveling, so it is important to be sure the horse leaves home well hydrated.

If possible, weigh the horse the day transport will begin. For comparison, weigh 2 large sacks of feed and record their weights. Keep the sacks intact to weigh on the scale at your destination. You will then be able to compare departure with arrival weights, compensating for differences in scale accuracy.

■ Familiarization to confinement and training to load

Individual horse responses to the confinement of a transport vehicle vary greatly. Some horses adjust well to the shipping environment while others may not. Lack of adjustment may be reflected in a persistently increased heart rate and high concentrations of stress hormones such as cortisol and ACTH, and nervous or anxious behavior during transport. Observation suggests that horses that are experienced travelers often are more relaxed than first time travelers. Training to load quietly on the transport vehicle and to accept forced confinement prior to long journeys may be extremely helpful in decreasing the stress of transport. If possible, familiarize the horse with the actual transport vehicle to be used. Encourage the horse to drink and eat while confined in the transport vehicle. If the horse must be transported alone, train the horse to stand quietly by itself in the transport vehicle.

When co-mingling, especially with unfamiliar horses, will be required, such as during air transport or in a large commercial van, it is important to be sure that the horse's temperament will allow shipping under these circumstances. Fractious or aggressive horses are dangerous to themselves and to other horses in the transport vehicle. Suitable physical or chemical restraint may be required for safe transport of such horses. Effectiveness of methods of restraint for anxious or aggressive horses should be tested by the owner before the journey begins.

■ Competent handlers

Make sure that shipping arrangements include provision for an adequate number of competent handlers to manage horses in large road transport vehicles or airplanes. Especially during air transport, it is essential to have highly experienced handlers familiar with managing ill, nervous, or aggressive horses during flight. The Animal Air Transport Association (AATA US Office, c/o Nonprofit Services Corp., 10700 Richmond Ave., Suite 201, Houston, TX 77042) has introduced a certification process for competence of handlers accompanying horses during air travel. When possible, it is advisable to have a handler familiar with the group of horses.

■ Medications

Administration of any medication can result in an adverse reaction, and a veterinarian should always be consulted before medication is given to a horse that must travel. All unnecessary medications should be avoided before travel. In particular, corticosteroids (*i.e.* dexamethasone or prednisone) and nonsteroidal anti-inflammatory drugs (NSAID) (*i.e.* aspirin, phenylbutazone, flunixine meglumine, indomethacin, meclofenamic acid) should be avoided. Corticosteroids may depress the horse's immune responses to bacterial invasion of the respiratory tract, and NSAIDs mask febrile responses to infection and may potentiate gastric ulcer formation. Indiscriminate use of antimicrobial agents such as penicillin, gentocin, or potentiated sulfa drugs should be avoided as these drugs may alter gastrointestinal flora and predispose to colitis and diarrhea. Administration of one dose of prophylactic antibiotics before shipping is not recommended at this time.

Unfortunately, there are currently no data concerning the use of immunomodulators, such as interferon, pre-transport. Although efficacy has not yet been scientifically demonstrated, there are anecdotal accounts of beneficial effects of interfreon-alpha and further study is needed. The use of immunostimulating drugs (*i.e.* EquiStim, Equimune IV) should be avoided as these drugs may induce fever and malaise difficult to distinguish from shipping fever. Additionally, beneficial effects of immunostimulants have not been proven in horses during transport.

For many years, laxatives such as mineral oil have been administered prophylactically before transport to many horses. This practice is acceptable, but not usually essential.

Sedation may be required for loading difficult horses or during the first part of the journey. A veterinarian's advice should always be sought when selecting sedative drugs and designing a dosing regimen. The use is not the case, (*i.e.* foals or yearlings) shipping boots or bandages may be a liability instead of an asset. Train the horse to wear protective bandages if you plan to use them. Remove shoes for shipping if appropriate. Blankets should be appropriate for the temperature expected in the vehicle.

■ Recovery period

Despite every effort at preventing shipping fever or other transport-related disease, some horses will become ill during or within the first the 3 days following transport. It is advisable to plan for a convalescent period of at least 3 days after shipping to allow for treatment of horses that may be ill. As treatment in the post-shipping period may require the use of drugs forbidden during competiton, a period of 7 or 8 days between arrival and competiton is preferable.

DURING TRANSPORT

■ Duration of journey

Journeys of 3 hours or less are unlikely to be associated with transport related diseases, physiologic derangements such as dehydration, or fatigue due to energy expenditure and reduced feed intake. It is unnecessary to plan rest or observation stops for such short journeys.

Ground transport time per day should not exceed approximately 12 hours from the time the first horse is loaded on the vehicle. After 12 hours of transport, horses should be removed from the vehicle and comfortably stabled for at least 8 hours. Long hauls should be punctuated by long rest periods. Short breaks during a long haul are not restful for horses and may be harmful if horses are required to stand in a suboptimally ventilated and hot vehicle, restrained with the head up, during short rest periods. Even when horses are unloaded from the transport vehicle, short breaks do not allow sufficient time to rest from the exertion of postural adjustments to transport, or to clear mucus from the airways. We recommend briefly checking horses approximately every 4 hours during long journeys.

■ Feed and water

Palatable water should be offered regularly (approximately every 4 hours) during prolonged ground or plane transport. If possible, it may be advisable to carry water, especially for horses that are reluctant to consume water that is not from the home source.

It is important that horses eat during long journeys. However, it is also imperative that the environment on the transport vehicle have as little contamination of the air with respirable particles as possible. In particular, the breathing zone around the horse's muzzle should not be heavily contaminated with particulate matter. Because hay nets must be placed very close to (or within) the breathing zone, it is essential that hay be as dust free as possible. It is therefore recommended that hay be thoroughly soaked in water before being loaded on the vehicle or fed in a net to horses. Hay cubes are an alternative source of forage, and can be moistened prior to feeding if needed. Another alternative to conventional hay is haylage. Haylage contains little dust, is nutritious and palatable. Although suppliers of haylage may be difficult to find, one source is Tri-Forage Farms Ltd. RR#2, Bath Ontario KOH 1GO Canada. (www.triforage.com). However, it is never advisable to radically change a horse's diet before transport. Therefore, if haylage is not routinely fed, this product should be gradually introduced into the diet in the 2 weeks before transport.

Conventional wisdom suggsts that the amount of grain in the diet should be reduced immediately before, during, and for several days after transport. Gastrointestinal stasis may be associated with transport and grain feeding may predispose to colic. In addition, energy requirements during transport are substantially reduced as compared to requirements for training or competing. During overnight rest stops grain rations should be fed at no more than half the usual measure. The necessity of reducing grain intake during transport requires further study.

The weight of hay and grain consumed by each horse during transport should be monitored. Inexpensive, portable small scales are readily available. Weigh feed offered to the horse and then weigh the uncomsumed portions. See *sample monitoring forms for road and air transport*, on pages 30 - 34.

■ Head posture
Horses should be given as much freedom of movement of their heads as is safe. Restraint in the head up posture for prolonged intervals may severely compromise pulmonary (lung) clearance mechanisms and predispose to shipping fever. Hay nets should be placed as low as possible while still assuring that horses cannot entangle their feet in the nets.

■ Bedding
Bedding is a major source of respirable particles in the air of the transport vehicle. Bedding should be as dust free and absorbent as possible. In general, it is best to avoid straw, sawdust and shavings. Paper or corrugated cardboard bedding are recommended. Bedding should be kept to the minimal amount needed to absorb urine and fecal fluids. If possible, soiled bedding should be removed at rest and watering stops. This practice is not feasible on large vans or in aircraft.

■ Ambient conditions and transport vehicle environment

Avoid road transport during hot, humid weather. If transport is essential under such conditions, it is imperative to minimize time when horses are standing in a stationary vehicle, as temperature and humidity in the vehicle will probably exceed the ambient conditions outside the vehicle. Windows and scoops for ventilation should be open at all times to keep conditions within the transport vehicle as comfortable as possible. If the vehicle is stationary for more than a few minutes, such as if a breakdown occurs, consider using an auxiliary ventilation system such as multiple fans, or, when possible, unload horses while repairs are completed. Do not ship horses in blankets during hot weather. If horses are sweating under blankets during transport, remove the blankets. Overheating is more dangerous to horses than cold.

Shipping during periods of climatic extremes or when major shifts in temperature are expected should be avoided. Horses tolerate cold better than extreme heat. The risk of overheating during transport is more dangerous and a much more common thermoreugulatory problem for horses than is the potential of diffficulties (illness, injuries) associated with cold conditions. When shipping in extremely cold weather, do not clip horses before shipping, and ship with adequate blankets. Check under blankets frequently to be sure horses are not sweating. The greater the stocking density on the transport vehicle, the more heat will be generated by the horses themselves. If horses are sweating under blankets during transport, remove the blankets. Do not ship horses in blankets during hot weather.

■ Monitoring during transport

During long (> 6 hour) road transport or any air transport, horses should be monitored frequently (every 4 hours). During air transport, horses should be observed hourly if possible (Figure 4). Sample monitoring forms for road and air transport are included on pages 30 - 34. It is important to rapidly identify horses that are developing shipping fever during transport. Therapeutic intervention during air travel may be life saving, and will decrease recovery times after arrival. It is strongly recommended that a veterinarian always accompany horses during air travel. Horses that become ill during road transport should be removed from the transport environment as quickly as possible. This may necessitate leaving a horse at a veterinary hospital en route. This alternative is preferable to continuing transport and risking development of severe pneumonia and/or pleuritis. Fever, (>38.3°C 101°F for adult, or > 38.9°C, 102°F for foal < 6 months of age), depression, inappetance, nasal discharge, and/or cough should prompt intervention. Frequent moni-

Figure 4: *Horses confined in air-stables for transport. Note the utilization of almost all free space in the aircraft by the air-stables. Horse can be observed through the air-stable windows; however, access may be somewhat limited. Photograph courtesy of Dr. Mark Ravenaugh*

toring also allows identification of horses with other problems such as colic, dehydration, or injury.

Inappetant horses or horses that will not drink during transport are at increased risk of developing shipping fever and may require a prolonged recovery period after shipping. Such horses can be treated with fluids (*i.e.* intravenous or nasogastric) during air journeys or at long rest stops during long road transport.

■ Treatment of horses with shipping fever during air transport

During air transport, rapid identification and expediant initiation of treatment by a veterinarian of shipping fever will likely lessen the severity of disease and facilitate more rapid recovery of affected horses. All antibiotics mentioned here require parenteral administration by a veterinarian. Controlled studies assessing efficacy of treatment regimens are lacking; however, ceftiofur has been used successfully by Dr Leadon. Based on the likelihood of envolvement of a streptococcal organism in shipping fever, other potentially useful anitbiotics include potassium penicillin intravenously every 6 hours, sodium penicillin intravenously or intramuscularly every 6 hours, or sodium ampicillin intravenously or intramuscularly every 6 hours. To provide more broad spectrum coverage, gentamicin, given once every 24 hours intravenously or intramuscularly, may be added to penicillin or ampicillin therapy.

■ Restraint and sedation

Nervous or fractious horses must be adequately restrained or sedated during transport. It is very helpful to identify such horses before transport so that adequate provision can be made for sedation during transport, and for veterinary assistance if required. It is strongly recommended that a veterinarian always be present during air transport of horses. A plan for co-mingling of horses should be made to minimize behavioral problems.

AFTER TRANSPORT

■ Expected condition on arrival

Horses that travel well will be bright and alert with a normal rectal temperature upon arrival at their destination. They should voluntarily drink and be keenly interested in eating within 1 or 2 hours of arrival (Leadon 1990). Hand walking or turn out in a small paddock for an hour or so upon arrival after a long journey is recommended. Hay can be fed ad libitum and grain should be gradually reintroduced into the diet over the ensuing 2 days. Grain should be limited or excluded from the diet of horses that become ill during transport.

■ Monitoring

Rectal temperature should be recorded morning and evening. When possible, weigh horses upon arrival and then daily at the same time for the next 3 to 7 days. Comparison with a pre-transport weight (if available) is useful to quantify actual weight losses and to assess the effects of shipping. To account for differences in scales at departure and destination sites, weigh the same 2 or 3 sacks of feed (at least 45 kg/sack) on both sets of scales. Determine the increment difference in weight on the destination scale, and adjust horse arrival weights accordingly. Horses that become ill during transport may experience greater weight loss than those that remain healthy. The rate of return of body weight to the pre-transport baseline value may provide an index of recovery from transport. Note that fluid deficits due to dehydration during transport will be replaced (by horses that drink adequately) within the first 24 hours after arrival. Return of body mass requires a longer interval after transport. Horses with transport-associated diseases may have slower weight gains than healthy horses during the recovery period.

Horses with signs of shipping fever, such as fever, nasal discharge, cough, depression and inappetance, will be readily identified by this monitoring system. It is important to remember that some horses will not show signs of shipping fever until 2 to 3 days after transport

(Leadon 1990). Occasionally, horses may have colic or diarrhea after shipping. Seek veterinary assistance immediately if transport-associated disease is suspected.

■ Recovery times

A specified recovery interval should be part of the pre-shipment plan for horses making long journeys. For trips <6 hours, 30 minutes hand walking and provision of an opportunity to drink and relax in a paddock or stall for several hours are all that may be required. For road journeys of 6 to 12 hours, a one day rest period is likely to be sufficient. When horses travel >12 hours by road or are transported by plane, a recovery period of 2 to 3 days should be planned. Recovery of pre-transport weight may require more than 2 to 3 days. Horses that have transport-associated diseases may require 7 days or more to recover. Because it is likely, based on currently available data, that a percentage of horses making long road or air journeys will develop shipping fever, it is recommended that an interval of 7 to 8 days be allowed for recovery to accommodate treatment of those horses that become ill. In addition a 7 to 8 day recovery period allows time for clearance of medications necessary for treatment of disease but not allowed by the medication rules of the competition for which the horse has been shipped.

■ Return journey

The effects of shipping are likely to be cumulative. Horses should be allowed 1 to 5 days (time commensurate with effort) to recover from the competition. It is highly desirable that horses be rested and relaxed before shipping home.

HEALTH STATUS OF HORSES DURING GROUND TRANSPORT: GREATER THAN 6 HOURS DURATION: DAY 1

Date_____

■ Horse Identification
Name_____
Age_____ Breed_____
Sex: Fe M G
Owner Name_____
Address_____

■ Journey Information
Departure Location_____
Destination_____
Date & time:
  First horse loaded_____
  This horse loaded_____
  Last horse loaded_____
Date & time of unloading_____
Location_____

■ Horse History
Most recent travel experience:
  ___ Short Haul (<3 hours)
  ___ Intermediate Haul (6 - 12 hours)
  ___ Long Haul (>12 hours)
  Date_____
Vaccinations Current:
  Flu___ EHV 1/4___ Strangles___
  Other:_____
History of recent illness:
Date/Description/Treatment_____

■ PreTravel Veterinary Examination
T_____ P_____ R_____ CRT_____
Auscultation of Chest_____
Auscultation of Abdomen_____
Body Weight (kg - lb)_____
Attitude Assessment:
  Depressed (**D**)
  Bright/Alert/Resposive (**BAR**)
  Anxious (**A**)
  Nervous/Fractious (**NF**)
Hydration: ___ Normal
  ___ Dehydrated (6 8%)
Position in Trailer:
  Two horse: ❏ Right ❏ Left
  Slant load: ❏ Front ❏ Middle ❏ Back
  Large van: ❏ Facing front ❏ Facing back
  Position with respect to other horses:
    ❏ Outside ❏ Middle
  Total number of horses on vehicle:_____

■ Monitoring During Travel:
Time of Departure_____ (0 hr)

Hours ▸▸▸▸	0	4	8	12*
Attitude Code				
Rectal temp (Q 8hr)				
RR (Q 8hr)				
HR (Q 8hr)				
Cough (Q 4hr)				
Nasal Discharge (Q 4hr)				
Water Intake (L-gal) (Q 4hr)				
Hay Intake (kg - lb) Q 12hr)				
Grain Intake (kg - lb) Q 12hr)				
Ambient Temp (Q 4hr)				
Humidity (Q 4hr)				

* 12 hours or hour (___) after start when unloaded for long rest

Sedation: Drug/Dose/Route_____ Time administered_____
Treatment: Drug/Dose/Route_____ Time administered_____
Describe indications & effect of treatment_____
Arrival Condition: Body weight (kg - lb)_____ BAR Depressed Sick (**SEEK VETERINARY ASSISTANCE**)
Signs of illness_____

30

HEALTH STATUS OF HORSES DURING GROUND TRANSPORT: GREATER THAN 6 HOURS DURATION: DAY 2 & FOLLOWING

Date_____

■ Horse Identification

Name_____
Age_____ Breed_____ Sex: Fe M G
Body Weight (kg - lb)_____
Attitude Assessment:
Depressed (**D**) Bright/Alert/Responsive (**BAR**) Anxious (**A**) Nervous/Fractious (**NF**)

■ Monitoring During Travel:
Time of Departure_____ (0 hr)

Hours → ↑ ↑ ↑ ↑ ↑	0	4	8	12*
Attitude Code				
Rectal temp (Q 8hr)				
RR (Q 8hr)				
HR (Q 8hr)				
Cough (Q 4hr)				
Nasal Discharge (Q 4hr)				
Water Intake (L-gal) (Q 4hr)				
Hay Intake (kg - lb) Q 12hr				
Grain Intake (kg - lb) Q 12hr				
Ambient Temp (Q 4hr)				
Humidity (Q 4hr)				

HOURS AFTER DEPARTURE

* 12 hours or hour (___) after start when unloaded for long rest

Sedation: Drug/Dose/Route_____ Time administered_____
Treatment: Drug/Dose/Route_____ Time administered_____
Describe indications & effect of treatment_____
Arrival Condition: Body weight (kg - lb)_____ BAR   Depressed   Sick (**SEEK VETERINARY ASSISTANCE**)
Signs of illness_____

■ Position in Trailer
Two horse: ❏ Right ❏ Left
Slant load: ❏ Front ❏ Middle ❏ Back
Large van: ❏ Facing front ❏ Facing back
Position with respect to other horses:
❏ Outside ❏ Middle
Total number of horses on vehicle:___

■ Journey Information
Intermediate Stop Location_____

Time loaded:
First horse_____
This horse_____
Last horse_____
Time Departed_____

31

HEALTH STATUS OF HORSES DURING AIR TRANSPORT: FIRST TAKE OFF

Date___

■ Horse Identification
Name___
Age___ Breed___
Sex: Fe M G
Owner Name___
Address___

■ Journey Information
Departure Location___
Destination___
Date & time loaded into airstable___
Elapsed time in airstable before take off (hours)___
Date & time of landing___
Time horse unloaded from airstable___

■ Horse History
Length of Journey to Airport (hours)___
Total # of flights previously taken___
Most recent travel experience:
___ Short Flight (<3hours)
___ Intermediate Flight (4 - 10 hours)
___ Long Flight (>10 hours)
Date___
Vaccinations Current:
Flu___ EHV 1/4___ Strangles___
Other:___
History of recent illness:
Date/Description/Treatment

■ In flight Monitoring: Time of take off_____ (0 hr)
(Use new grid for every take off)

Hours	0	1	2	3	4	5	6	7	8	9	10	11	12	13	14	15	16	17	18
Visual Ok (Q 1 hr)																			
Rectal temp (Q 6hr)																			
RR (Q 6hr)																			
HR (Q 6hr)																			
Cough (Q 1hr)																			
Nasal Discharge (Q 1 hr)																			
Water Intake (L-gal) (Q 6 hr)																			
Hay Intake (kg - lb) Q 6hr)																			
Grain Intake (kg - lb) Q 6hr)																			
Ambient Temp (Q 4 hr)																			
Humidity (Q 4hr)																			

■ PreTravel Veterinary Examination
T___ P___ R___ CRT___
Auscultation of Chest___
Auscultation of Abdomen___
Body Weight (kg - lb)___
Attitude Assessment:
Depressed (**D**)
Bright/Alert/Resposive (**BAR**)
Anxious (**A**)
Nervous/Fractious (**NF**)

Sedation: Drug/Dose/Route_____ Time administered___
Treatment: Drug/Dose/Route_____ Time administered___
Describe indications & effect of treatment___
Arrival Condition: Body weight (kg - lb)___ BAR   Depressed   Sick (**SEEK VETERINARY ASSISTANCE**)
Signs of illness___

32

HEALTH STATUS OF HORSES DURING AIR TRANSPORT: GROUND STOPS

Date _____

■ **Horse Identification**

Name _____
Age ____ Breed ____
Sex: Fe M G

■ **Monitoring while on the ground:** Ground time (hrs) _____

Hours	0	1	2	3	4	5	6	7	8	9	10	11	12	13	14	15	16	17	18
Visual Ok (Q 1 hr)																			
Rectal temp (Q 6hr)																			
RR (Q 6hr)																			
HR (Q 6hr)																			
Cough (Q 1hr)																			
Nasal Discharge (Q 1hr)																			
Water Intake (L-gal) (Q 6 hr)																			
Hay Intake (kg - lb) Q 6hr)																			
Grain Intake (kg - lb) Q 6hr)																			
Ambient Temp (Q 4 hr)																			
Humidity (Q 4hr)																			

HOURS OF GROUND TIME

Sedation: Drug/Dose/Route _____ Time administered _____
Ground Stop Condition: Body weight (kg - lb) ____ BAR Depressed Sick
   Signs of illness _____
Treatment: Drug/Dose/Route _____ Time administered _____
   Comments _____

33

Torikai 1996), elevations in heart rate (Clark *et al.* 1993, Waran 1993, Waran *et al.* 1993, Smith *et al.* 1994a, 1994b, Waran and Cuddeford 1995) and energy expenditure (Doherty *et al.* 1997), increased concentrations of plasma cortisol (Baucus *et al.* 1990b, White *et al.* 1991, Clark *et al.* 1993) and ACTH (Takagi *et al.* 1995), serum biochemical changes (Codazza *et al.* 1974, Leadon 1989, Leadon *et al.* 1990, White *et al.* 1991), increased progesterone concentrations and embryonic death in pregnant mares (Baucus *et al.* 1990b), fluid and electrolyte imbalances (White *et al.* 1991, Friend *et al.* 1998, van den Berg *et al.* 1998), diarrhea (Owen *et al.* 1983, McClintock and Begg 1990), reactivation of *Salmonella* infection (Owen *et al.* 1983), azoturia (Cregier 1982) and/or rhabdomyolysis (Ito *et al.* 1992), and pulmonary infections, commonly known as "shipping fever" (Cregier 1982, Hayakawa *et al.*1993, Oikawa *et al.* 1994, 1995, Momoi *et al.* 1996, Raidal *et al.* 1997).

Road transport is a complex operation involving multiple potentially stressful components. These include separation from a familiar environment, isolation, confinement, vibration, jolting, accelerations and decelerations, loss of balance, noise, fluctuations of temperature and humidity, altered and possibly inadequate ventilation, exposure to gases and particles from exhaust, urine and feces, deprivation of food and water, orientation in relation to the direction of travel in the horse box, length of journey, method of transport, skill of the driver, and head posture. As a result, it is difficult *a priori* to judge which of these components (if any) is/are primarily responsible for the physiological and pathological changes that have been associated with road transport (Leadon 1994, Waran and Cuddeford 1995).

In this review we consider potential sources of stress within the land, road or surface transport environment, the effects of road transit and its associated stress on the health of athletic horses, predisposing factors for equine respiratory disease associated with transportation by road, and methods that might be used for specific early diagnosis of equine respiratory disease associated with transportation, *e.g.*, ELISA for equine pulmonary surfactant protein and changes in pulmonary clearance rates using nuclear scintigraphy. We emphasize, in particular, studies that have been conducted in Japan by the Japan Racing Association (JRA) that may not be familiar to occidental researchers.

■ Limitations to comparing transport studies

Before considering specific findings of studies directed toward understanding mechanisms causing and biological responses of horses to road transport stress, we must emphasize several serious limitations to the available data and the ability to compare those data meaningfully. First of all, transport vehicles, management protocols, and ambient environmental conditions vary so markedly that direct comparison of results between studies is very problematic. Indeed, road transport can result in findings as different as significant elevations of serum cortisol concentration (Clark *et al.* 1993, Smith *et al.* 1996a) vs. no change (Ferlazzo *et al.* 1984). Whether such differences result from differences in the assay sensitivities between laboratories, experimental protocols, populations of horses studied, or other reasons is often difficult to determine. The findings of any given study may be limited to a very defined transport situation, and generalization of results may not be warranted. Even within a single study, it may be impossible to control climatic variation from one experimental replicate to the next, increasing within-treatment variation markedly, and decreasing statistical power to detect differences.

A second problem in comparing studies of transport stress experiments is that similar studies utilize very differently-defined controls, thereby affecting the interpretation as to what the experimental hypothesis was actually testing. For example, in studies of the effects of motion and orientation within the vehicle (head forward or backward) during transport on heart rate, some studies define the control as the horse standing in its stall, others as the animal tethered, and others as the animal in the vehicle restrained in the same manner and orientation as during transport, but without the vehicle in motion. These different approaches result in one experiment evaluating the hypothesis that restraint + confinement in the vehicle + motion (with its correlates, *e.g.*, noise, etc.) affect heart rate, a second experiment evaluating the effects of confinement + motion, and the third experiment evaluating only the effects of motion. Significant differences in interpretation of findings can result simply from these fundamental differences in experimental approach.

Yet another limitation to interpreting the results of road transport experiments is that, because of the high cost of conducting the studies (particularly if balanced designs with randomized orders of presentation are used), sample sizes tend to be small, in the range of three to 30 animals per study. This presents a fundamental problem in that individual variation in responses makes it difficult to separate signal from noise in evaluating the effects of an experimental perturbation. Indeed, caution must be used in not overgeneralizing the results of such studies, as individual animals may have preferences that are significant in terms of their stress response, but different from the majority of the population.

POTENTIAL STRESSORS DURING TRANSPORT

Transport-related stress is likely to be multifactorial in origin due to the diverse nature of the environmental stressors that may occur during transport. Confinement, movement, noise, lack of previous exposure/experience, and the presence of exhaust or other gases, coupled with changes in air temperature, relative humidity, and the number of airborne microorganisms, are all potential sources of stress in the transport environment (Leadon 1994). In the most general sense, we can consider stress-related factors to fall into four broad categories:

1. *Environmental* - factors such as temperature, humidity, season, day length/time of day, and ambient air quality (dust, air pollutants);
2. *Vehicle design* - factors that are related to the characteristics of the transport vehicle, such as ventilation (effects of window and vent placement), recirculation of interior gases, insulation and noise (sound intensity and quality), visual cues, suspension and its effect on vibration, and accelerations and decelerations;
3. *Management during transport* - factors such as frequency and duration of stops, feeding and watering, method by which horses are restrained in the vehicle (head height, direction), and skill of the driver;
4. *Biological responses* - the physiological responses of individual horses to the above stressors, potentially influenced by such factors as sex, age, prior shipping experience, socialization with surrounding horses, reproductive status, vaccination status, and prior or subsequent exposure to potential pathogens and/or non-transport stressors.

Some environmental factors (*i.e.*, weather, many biological factors) may be beyond the ability of the shipper to modify; others, particularly management factors, some related to vehicle design, and selected biological factors (*i.e.*, vaccination status and familiarization with the transport vehicle), may be amenable to modification to minimize the stress experienced and subsequent response of the horse. We summarize findings from a number of studies related to the factors listed above.

■ Vibration and oscillation

During vehicular transportation, horses experience a variety of different environmental changes from their daily lives. In particular, vibration and oscillation are only experienced when the horse is being transported, and they continue throughout a road transport episode. These variables might stress a horse being transported, however, little published research has defined the magnitudes and frequencies of vibration and oscillation to which a horse is subjected, or their effects on the horse.

The Japan Racing Association (JRA) has conducted studies (unpublished data) in which accelerometers were positioned to measure and analyze the magnitudes and frequencies of oscillation in 18-horse road transport vans over a period of 16 h. Accelerometers were oriented along the longitudinal axis of the vehicle (x-axis, backward and forward), the vertical axis (z-axis, upward and downward), and laterally (y-axis, to the right- and left-hand sides; vehicles in Japan travel on the left side of the road). The averages of the maximum oscillations in acceleration are shown in Figure 1.

The magnitudes of acceleration along all three axes in the vehicle in motion exceeded the limits of allowable values for vehicle vibration in humans (0.2 g). Moreover, histogram analysis of these accelerations demonstrated that the frequency of maximum oscillations was lower for expressways than for public roads, indicating there were fewer maximum oscillations or movements during transportation on expressways. Simultaneous measurements were made of oscillations during 30 min of transport on public roads and expressways and the heart rates of

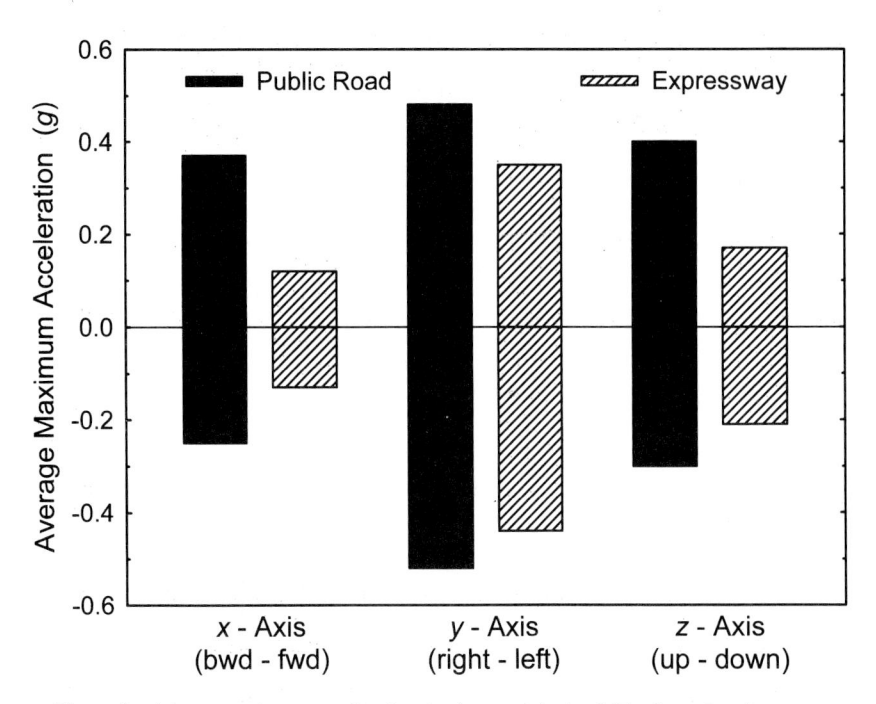

Figure 1: *Average maximum accerlerations in three axes during 16 h of transport in an 18-horse van on roads in Japan. Solid bars are data from public roads, hatched bars are data from expressways.*

three horses. Heart rate and accelerations in the x-, y-, and z-axes were significantly and positively correlated (unpublished data). Respiratory rates increased during the course of transport, yet decreased to nearly pre-transport values while at a stop (Hobo *et al.* 1995). These results suggest that vibration and oscillation during transport have the potential to act as a stressor.

Smith *et al.* (1996b) evaluated differences in vibration in a two-horse trailer by evaluating the root mean squares of accelerations produced in the z-axis in the suspension, trailer frame, hooves of horses being transported, and their thoraxes. They evaluated the effects of different suspension and tire combinations, as well as speeds and road surfaces (smooth vs. "rough," using metal cables stretched across the road surface to provide a controlled and uniform roughness). They found that the natural frequencies of oscillation of the trailer were near those of the horses' bodies, a combination that results in fatigue in humans. Additionally, they found that slower speeds and smoother roads produced less vibration, and that modification of the trailer's suspension and tires significantly affected the vibration transmitted to the horse. However, in a related study, they reported that changing the trailer suspension to provide different vibration characteristics did not detectably affect heart rates, serum cortisol concentrations, nor pulmonary clearance rates of ^{99m}Tc-DTPA in 24 h transport experiments (Smith *et al.* 1996a).

■ Transport vehicle interior environment

Leadon *et al.* (1990) suggested that confinement of horses within their stalls may lead to contamination of their immediate environment with microorganisms. A large number of airborne microorganisms present in the transport vehicle during transportation could be inhaled, thereby inducing respiratory disease. He also suggested the possibility that the desiccating effects of exposure to dry air while in a vehicle (particularly aircraft) in motion may result in diminished mucosal clearance mechanisms in the airways (Leadon 1994).

Oikawa *et al.* (1995) reported measurements of the transport vehicle interior environment during a 41 h journey. Horses were loaded four to a truck, had free access to hay throughout the journey and were offered water during rest periods. In this study, the concentration of ammonia gas emitted from the build up of excreta in the vehicle increased in proportion to the duration of transport. There was no relation between atmospheric dust concentration and travel time, although atmospheric dust concentration increased when each horse ate hay. For humans during work, the permitted concentration of atmospheric ammonia is 25 ppm, and 8 mg/m^3 for atmospheric dust concentration (Smith *et al.* 1996a). Although the ammonia and dust concentrations obtained during this study were lower than those permitted for humans, if the horses were exposed to these gases or dust particles for an extended period in an environment in which they were subjected to other stressors associated with road transport, it is possible they could contribute to adverse respiratory system effects.

To clarify the effects of inspired aerial ammonia on the respiratory tract during vehicular transport, an experiment was conducted on three healthy thoroughbred horses (4 yr old) that were free from respiratory diseases (Katayama *et al.* 1995). One horse (No.1) was exposed to ammonia gas at concentrations of 2-17 ppm, which is the same range of concentration as in a transport vehicle during transport The second horse (No.2) was exposed to concentrations of 40-130 ppm, which is the maximum allowable exposure concentration for humans. The third horse (No.3) served as the control without any exposure to ammonia gas; exposure time was 40 h. The exposed horses demonstrated clinical signs of coughing and hypersecretion of nasal discharge, but had no significant hematological changes. Morphologically, a slight swelling of the tips of cilia in the tracheal epithelium was observed in horse No.1. Horse No.2 showed marked changes in the form of lost cilia and degenerative cytoplasmic changes of the tracheal epithelium (Katayama *et al.* 1995). These observations suggest that changes in the atmospheric environment of the vehicle during road transport may have significant effects over time that contribute to stress and a physiological response.

Smith *et al.* (1999) evaluated the effects of different combinations of windows and vents on the washout of gases from an enclosed two-horse trailer. They found that retention of gases in the trailer can be modified by altering the flow environment into and out of the trailer, particularly by opening and closing the doors at the rear of the trailer. However, minimal changes in interior air flow pattern and washout resulted from opening and closing of windows and vents.

■ Head posture during road transport

The common practice of tying horses by their halters in transport vehicles (Figure 2) has the potential to act as a stressor and contribute to the development of transport-associated respiratory disease. There is some evidence that head posture during transport has an influence on tracheal mucociliary clearance function in horses (Racklyeft and Love 1990, Raidal *et al.* 1995, Raidal *et al.* 1996). These studies showed that horses confined with their heads elevated for 24 h developed an accumulation of purulent airway secretions, increased numbers of bacteria

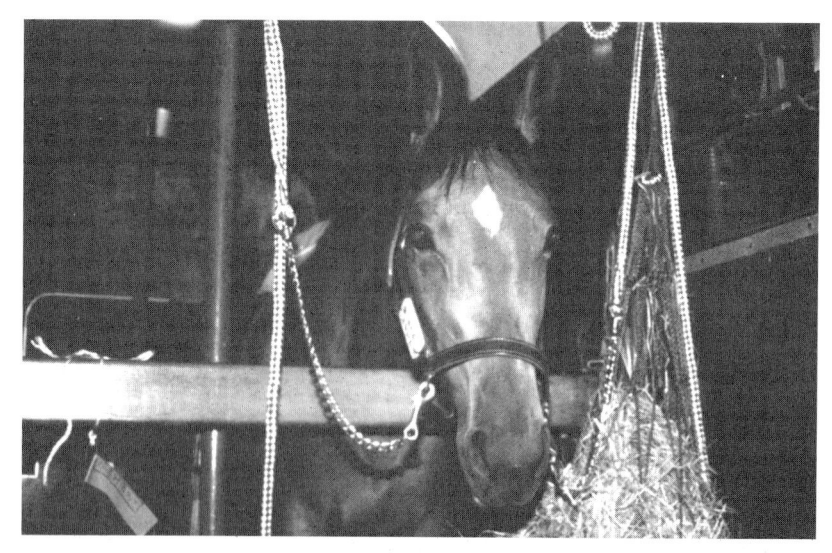

Figure 2: *Horses are typically tied with their heads elevated in a transport vehicle. Studies have shown that tying a horse's head in an elevated position for an extended period of time decreases airway clearance and increases concentrations of bacteria in the lower airways, possibly contributing to the development of "shipping fever" pneumonia. Photograph courtesy of the JRA.*

in the lower respiratory tract and decreased tracheal mucociliary clearance when compared with horses positioned with their heads lowered. These findings suggest that restraint of horses with their heads in an elevated position (cross-tying) during long journeys could contribute to the pathogenesis of lower respiratory tract diseases.

■ Orientation of the horse within the transport vehicle

Anecdotal evidence suggests that rear-facing horses in transport vehicles may be more relaxed than those that are forward-facing. A number of researchers have suggested that transporting horses restrained facing away from the direction of transport (head backward) might reduce accelerations and decelerations of their centers of mass and increase their stability (Cregier 1982, Clark *et al.* 1993, Waran 1993, Smith *et al.* 1994*a*, 1994*b*, Kusunose and Torikai 1996, Waran *et al.* 1996).

Cregier hypothesized that horses travel more comfortably and with less stress when facing away from the direction of travel, in part because they might better absorb shock and balance themselves by use of their hind limbs during deceleration; however, she provided no quantitative data to test the hypothesis (Cregier 1982). Smith *et al.* (1994a) tested Cregier's hypothesis by evaluating whether horses have lower heart rates, and presumably less stress, when facing backward versus forward in a trailer during road transport. They found that heart rates were not significantly different between horses facing forward or backward during transport, nor were they different between orientations while parked, although they were higher during transport than when parked. In contrast, Waran *et al.* (1996) reported that during transport average heart rate was significantly lower when horses were transported facing backward. They concluded that horses seemed to find being transported less physically stressful when facing backward than when facing forward. Most horses — but not all — placed in a transport vehicle without tethering preferred to face backward when the vehicle was in motion, but not when it was parked (Smith *et al.* 1994b, Kusunose and Torikai 1996). These results suggest that body orientation during transport may be a contributing stressor for many, although not necessarily all, horses.

PHYSIOLOGICAL RESPONSES INDUCED BY ROAD TRANSPORT

■ Body weight

Road transport has been reported to induce a number of physiological (Clark *et al.* 1993, Yamauchi *et al.* 1993, Hobo *et al.* 1995, Nambo *et al.* 1996, Friend *et al.* 1998) and behavioral (Cregier 1982, Clark *et al.* 1993, Waran 1993, Waran and Cuddeford 1995, Kusunose and Torikai 1996) changes in horses, including tachycardia (Clark *et al.* 1993, Waran 1993, Waran *et al.* 1993, Smith *et al.* 1994a, 1994b, Waran and Cuddeford 1995), postural shifts (Waran 1993) and diarrhea (Owen *et al.* 1983, McClintock and Begg 1990), in addition to changes in metabolic (White *et al.* 1991, Doherty *et al.* 1997, Friend *et al.* 1998), endocrine (Abott 1979, Baucus *et al.* 1990a, 1990b, Nambo *et al.* 1996) and biochemical parameters (Codazza *et al.* 1974, Leadon 1989, Leadon *et al.* 1990, White *et al.* 1991, Friend *et al.* 1998, Ishida *et al.* 1999). We summarize below some of these.

Reduced food and water intake have been observed in horses transported by road (Waran 1993). Waran reported that one day of road transport was associated with a 2.5% reduction in body weight, which was not regained until 2-3 days after transport (Waran 1993).

The fractional body weight loss for adult thoroughbred horses is related to transportation distance and traveling time. Experiments conducted either in the spring, summer, or fall, with temperatures ranging from 28 to 35°C and relative humidities from 61 to 91%, showed increases in weight loss with increasing time and distance of transport. (JRA unpublished data, Figure 3). Smith *et al.* (1996a) reported that for 24 hours of transport this weight loss stems from decreased feed and water intake while normal fecal output is maintained.

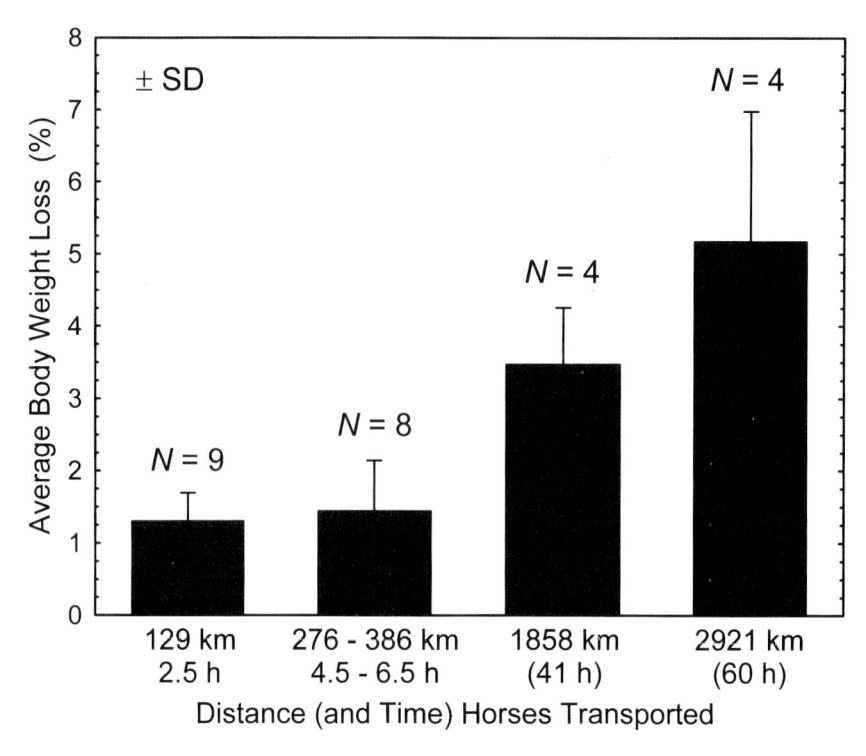

Figure 3: *Loss in body weight (percentage) in horses transported for different distances and durations during the spring, summer, or fall in Japan. Temperatures ranged from 28 - 35°C and relative humidities from 61 - 91%. N = number of horses per group.*

■ Endocrine

Previous studies have identified elevations in heart rate and increases in plasma concentrations of cortisol as indicative of a stress response evoked in horses by transportation (Clark *et al.* 1993, Smith *et al.* 1996a). The JRA (unpublished data) has measured heart rates at rest and during road transport continuously for 24 h via electrocardiograms in three groups: the first group was eight clinically healthy Thoroughbreds at rest in their stalls; the second group was five Thoroughbreds that did not experience pyrexia (fever) during transport; the third group was three Thoroughbreds that did experience pyrexia during transit. Mean heart rates over 24 h in each group were: 33.0 beat/min in the first group, 51.5 beat/min in the second group, and 61.1 beat/min in the third group, respectively. These results suggest that horses that develop pyrexia may have higher heart rates than those that do not. However, the results do not indicate if the higher heart rates were associated with horses experiencing greater stress that were more prone to becoming pyrexic, or whether the pyrexia induced the higher heart rates.

To evaluate possible relationships between stress and duration of transport, measurements were made of eight Thoroughbreds transported over 1,858 km for 41 h (Oikawa *et al.* 1995). Blood samples were collected prior to transportation by road, and every 5 h after departure. Adrenocorticotropic hormone (ACTH) and 11-hydroxycorticosteroid (11-OHCS) were measured as indices of stress; they reached their peaks within 5 h of the start of transport, suggesting that the horses experienced significant stress even during the initial period of transportation as compared to the later period (unpublished data). The concentrations decreased during the course of transportation in healthy horses, suggesting that the horses had either become accustomed to being transported or else had exhausted their supplies of these hormones. However, those horses affected with pyrexia (defined as rectal temperature greater than 38.6°C) *increased their concentrations* of ACTH and 11-OHCS with the onset of pyrexia, suggesting either that they experienced more prolonged or extreme stress or else that the pyrexia caused the increase in concentrations of these compounds. The onset of disease correlated with what might be interpreted as a degree of failure to adapt to being transported (unpublished data).

Transportation of acclimatized adult horses for 1 h in a trailer did not result in any changes in beta-endorphine concentrations (Leadon 1994). In contrast, Wi and Chen (1987) reported that transportation by road significantly increased plasma concentrations of beta-endorphin-like material (B-END-L1) from a basal value of 138 ± 12 to 196 ± 24 pg/ml within 30 min, and these concentrations were maintained at 45 min (177 ± 3 pg/ml). Plasma concentrations of B-END-L1 began to decline after 60 min of transport.

Cycling and pregnant mares had increased concentrations of plasma cortisol following transport (Baucus *et al.* 1990a, 1990b, Nambo *et al.* 1996). When mares in estrus were transported for 12 h, concentrations of plasma LH in the transported group were higher at the middle and end of transport when compared to those of a non-transported control group (Baucus *et al.* 1990a). Although stress may suppress the secretion of LH-releasing hormone and subsequent LH secretion via endogenous corticotropin-releasing hormone and opoid peptides, the pattern of LH secretion in mares in response to transport stress may depend on the estrous cycle (Baucus *et al.* 1990a). Similarly, Nambo *et al.* (1996) reported that, as a result of transporting three cycling mares in a trailer, basal secretion of LH was suppressed and the pattern of this suppression appeared to depend on the stage of the estrous cycle.

■ Respiratory, biochemical, and immune function

Transportation is generally recognized as a factor associated with an increased incidence of respiratory disorders in horses (Raphel and

Beech 1982, Mair and Lane 1989; Austin *et al.* 1995). However, the relationship between transport stress and changes in respiratory function of horses has yet to be clarified in many respects. Hobo *et al.* (1995) investigated respiratory patterns of horses during road transport using continuous measurements of respiratory rate via intratracheal pressure recording. Respiratory rates increased during the course of transport, yet decreased close to pre-transport values while at a stop. Arterial blood gases were not affected by increased ventilation during transport, and no significant changes occurred with the exception of mild hyperventilation in febrile horses. The tachypnea observed during transit was inferred not to be attributable to noises associated with the truck engine running, as the engine was kept running even during stops. However, the vibration of the truck in transit exceeded the limit of allowable values for vehicle vibration in humans (0.2 g). The investigators postulated that horses restrained in a small space within the truck might respond to the extraordinary vibration with an increase in respiratory rate, possibly via the proprioceptors of the limbs or via CNS excitation.

It is widely thought that a variety of stress factors acting on animals accelerate their production of superoxide (Ishida *et al.* 1999). Accordingly, athletic horses are considered to be exposed to a great deal of oxide stress due to transport. Ishida *et al.* (1999) evaluated the effects of transport on racehorses in terms of superoxide and antioxidative abilities by investigating changes in the superoxide-scavenging ability of equine serum using electron spin resonance (ESR). Changes in lipid peroxide concentrations that were being produced in equine serum by superoxide were also examined. Lipid peroxide concentrations increased as a result of transport. Coupled with this, the superoxide-scavenging ability of the serum declined during transport by road for 41 h. These results suggest that prolonged transport could result in the horse being exposed to a great amount of oxide stress.

There is little information on the influence of road transportation on equine cellular immune function (Anderson *et al.* 1985, Bayly *et al.* 1986 1997, Traub-Dargatz *et al.* 1988, Crisman *et al.* 1992, Raidal *et al.*). To evaluate this, 29 Thoroughbreds (3 yr old) had blood drawn before and immediately after arrival following shipping over 1,676 km during a 38 h interval (JRA unpublished data). Phagocytosis and lymphocyte subpopulations in peripheral blood were determined, as well as mitogen-induced blastogenesis of lymphocytes and nitroblue tetrazolium (NBT) reduction activity of neutrophils and pulmonary alveolar macrophages (PAM) that were collected by bronchoalveolar lavage

(BAL). During the journey, 12 of 29 (41%) horses transported were pyrexic. Both NBT reduction activity of neutrophils and lymphocyte blastogenesis activities tended to increase when measured immediately after arrival. Additionally, decreased T-lymphocyte and B-lymphocyte populations were observed, with the extent of T-cell depletion being marked. There seemed to be no significant difference in these indices between horses with pyrexia and those without pyrexia. PAM functions were not different in pyrexic vs. non-pyrexic horses.

Increased phagocytosis by equine PAM has been demonstrated following transportation (Crisman *et al.* 1992), but other researchers reported that transportation of 12 h duration did not alter the phagocytic function of PAM (Traub-Dargatz *et al.* 1988). Raidal *et al.* (1997) reported that six horses transported by road for 12 h experienced peripheral blood neutrophilia and a reduction in neutrophil phagocytic function evident for at least 36 h following transportation, suggesting that horses may require a number of days to recover normal immune response after the stress of transportation of this duration.

Although there are different findings with respect to peripheral leucocytes and PAM among researchers, the results described above suggest a significant alteration in peripheral blood lymphocyte and neutrophil functions, and possibly PAM ability during and after transport by road.

POST-TRANSPORT RECOVERY PERIOD

To determine an index of the post-transport recovery period, concentrations of horses' serum cortisol were measured during and after transport by road over a distance of 386 km (travel time 6 h) in four Thoroughbreds aged 3 to 6 yr old. During these measurements, the vehicle's interior was at 28 to 35°C, with a humidity of 61-78%. Serum cortisol concentrations were elevated immediately after transportation, but recovered to their initial pre-transport values within 15 h, as did body weights (JRA unpublished data). These results suggest that the stress response to transport of this duration is resolved during this interval.

■ Effects on subsequent athletic performance

Overall, transport in vehicles was found to have relatively little effect on subsequent athletic performance, as measured in time trials in eight Quarterhorses and Thoroughbreds transported for 8.1 km over 15 min, or for 194 km over a 2 to 2.5 h time period (Leadon 1994).

Codazza et al. (1974) reported a study of 40 clinically healthy Thoroughbreds aged 3 to 5 yr old that were transported for a distance of 300 km. They found that transportation over this distance had similar effects (after resting for 48 h) as a canter of 1,500 m on muscle function, with respect to changes in some serum enzyme activities and biochemical concentrations. They concluded that horses should be transported at least 48 h prior to a race to permit serum values to return to within the reference range. Transporting horses only 90 km had no significant effect on serum concentrations of sodium, potassium, chloride, glucose or total protein, or subsequent performance at submaximal exercise.

Similarly, 5 Thoroughbred racehorses, which had recently run races, were observed in order to assess the influence of transport on their athletic performance (Equine Research Institute, 1997). They were transported 129 km for 2.5 h at a vehicle temperature of 19 to 24°C. One week prior to the experiment (pre) and 2 h after transportation (post) they were run 1,900 m at a trot, 900 m at a canter, and then galloped for 1,400 m at a speed (12-13 m/s) similar to that achieved during actual races. Their running times and heart and respiratory rates pre- and post-transport are shown in Figure 4.

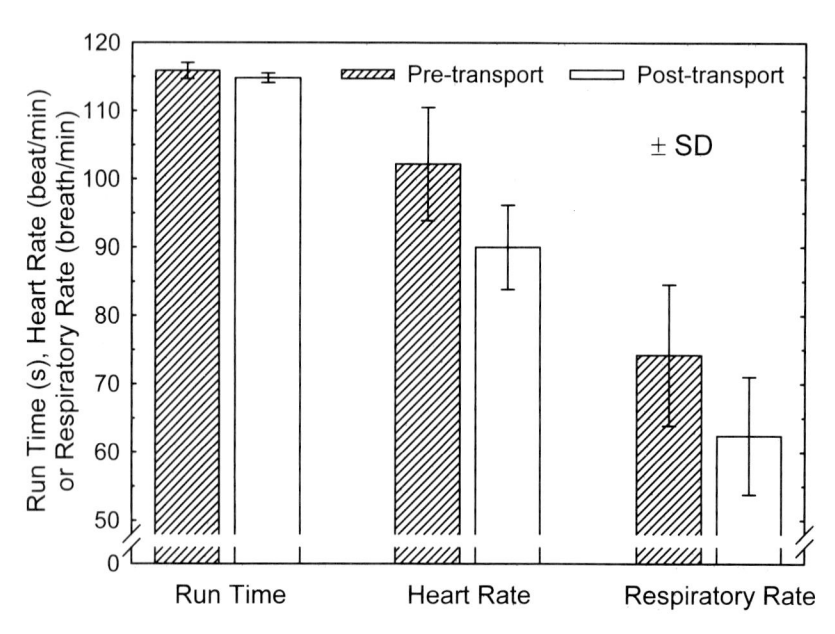

Figure. 4. *Effects of transporting five horses on running time (1,400m), heart rate (5 min post-gallop), and respiratory rate (end-gallop). Hatched bars are values measured when the horses were not transported, open bars are values measured one week later immediately after they were transported 129 km over 2.5 h.*

The data suggest that exercise performances of racehorses in daily race training and with road transport experience are not adversely affected by transport of less than 3 hours duration. Effects of road transport of longer duration on performance and the physiological response to exercise have not been assessed.

PATHOLOGICAL EFFECTS OF ROAD TRANSPORT

Transporting horses by road can produce various pathological changes, such as diarrhea, reactivating a prior *Salmonella* infection, azoturia, rhabdomyolysis, or so called "shipping fever," characterized by clinical signs such as depression, with the presence of soft cough, shallow frequent respirations, and febrile response. Of these pathological conditions, respiratory diseases, such as shipping fever, clinical pneumonia and/or pleuritis/pleuropneumonia complex, more commonly occur as a result of prolonged road transport. Little work has been done to evaluate the nature of these equine respiratory diseases associated with road transport and the pathogenesis of these diseases.

■ "Shipping fever" in horses

The term "shipping fever" is most commonly used at the present time to describe pneumonia in cattle caused by *Pasteurella haemolytica* (pneumonic Pasteurellosis), particularly in feedlot animals that have been through the stressful marketing process. However, this term was originally used for the pneumonia that commonly developed in horses shipped during World War I (Sinha and Abinanti 1962). Fifty years ago, or perhaps earlier, the term shipping fever was generally applied to a group of epizootic respiratory infections of horses that usually occurred after the shipment of young western horses eastward, or after the transfer of "green" country horses to city stables. Later, following extensive research, the "shipping fever complex" of horses was recognized as having three distinct etiologic agents, strangles, influenza, and contagious pneumonia (Sinha and Abinanti 1962).

Instead of the overly inclusive term of shipping fever, more appropriate terms for the respiratory conditions of horses developing either during or in the immediate post-travel period include equine transport pneumonia (Hayakawa *et al.* 1993), transportation-induced fever (Momoi *et al.* 1996), transport-associated respiratory disease (Raidal *et al.* 1997), pneumonia associated with transport (Oikawa *et al.* 1994) or equine respiratory disease occurring in association with transport (Oikawa *et al.* 1995).

way inflammation as a result of transport in two of the three affected horses (Oikawa et al. 1995). Similar observations have been made in horses with pre-existing mild respiratory infections. Such horses will frequently develop fulminating pleuropneumonia and eventually die if they are subjected to a period of prolonged transportation (Raphel and Beech 1982).

A consistent finding in the affected horses was focal serous neutrophilic pneumonia affecting the cranioventral portion of the caudal lung lobe with a propensity to affect the right lung. *Strep. z.* was isolated as the predominant organism from the pneumonic areas in which corresponding bacterial antigens were identified immunohistochemically. In addition to *Strep. z.*, other bacteria that were isolated included *alpha*-hemolytic *Streptococcus*, *Pasteurella* spp., *Escherihia coli*, *Staphylococcus* spp., *Enterococcus* spp. and *Bacillus* spp. Serological and viral cultures proved negative for respiratory viruses such as equine herpesvirus type I, equine adenovirus, equine rhinovirus type I and coronavirus.

Pathomorphologically, profuse migration of neutrophils, especially in the lumens of the alveolar capillaries, seemed to play an important role in the formation of the pneumonic lesions. Close association of neutrophils with the endothelial surface might lead to vascular damage, congestion of alveolar capillaries, increased capillary permeability, intra-alveolar effusion, and ischemic necrosis (coagulation necrosis of parenchyma in the lung). In other words, the initial lesion might develop from neutrophilic alveolitis, or inflammation of the alveolar capillary (microvasculitis) as a result of *Strep. z.* infection.

From a pathomorphological point of view, it is likely that transport adversely affected the normally effective mucosal defense mechanism in the airways, leading to invasion by *Strep. z.*, a common commensal organism in the equine tonsil and nasopharynx, into the lower airways, thus inducing acute lower airway inflammation in the affected horses. Evidence supporting this possibility includes increased mucus in the trachea after transport (Abott 1979), spread of *Strep. z.* from the upper to the lower trachea, where the organism would not normally be expected, associated with neutrophilic tracheitis (Anderson et al. 1985), tracheal ciliary abnormalities suggestive of impairment of mucociliary function in the airway (Austin et al.1995), and decreased amounts of secretory granules in goblet cells and the glandular epithelium of the trachea (decreased mucus lining) (Baucus et al. 1990b). It is noteworthy that causal organisms in these cases are not airborne microorganisms.

The normal equine tonsil is simultaneously colonized by multiple strains of *Strep. z.* expressing different protective M-like proteins (SzP). All SzP types found in normal tonsils were represented among the strains isolated from the tonsils of the horses that developed pneumonia. However, multiple isolates of *Strep. z.* from the lesions of individual cases of pneumonia secondary to transport had identical SzP, suggesting invasion by a single strain. This is consistent with the hypothesis that transit-associated respiratory diseases are endogenous opportunistic infections. Such infections could result from *Strep. z.* (originating in the palatine tonsil of the upper airway) multiplying when the horse is stressed, allowing invasion of the lower airway, and/or from decreased airway clearance due to mechanisms previously discussed, *i.e.*, head-tying. Invasion of the lower respiratory tract appears to involve single strains that are amplified under *in vivo* selection conditions that are as yet unknown (Timoney *et al.* 1997).

It has been reported that road transport can induce leukocytosis and neutrophilia, although the causal factors of this phenomenon still remain obscure. However, the fact that the numbers of peripheral leukocytes, especially neutrophils, are enhanced by longer transport distances may reflect a response to infection or epinephrine-induced neutrophilia (transient physiologic neutrophilia and/or corticosteroid-induced neutrophilia) (Yamauchi *et al.* 1993). Horses with clinical signs of shipping fever had pneumonic lesions suggesting that a microbial infection occurred in the affected horses.

In addition to the other effects of long-distance road transportation as described above, serum concentrations of granulocyte-colony stimulating factor (G-CSF) correlated positively with peak body temperatures and with increased peripheral neutrophil counts during transport (Momoi *et al.* 1996). Furthermore, a significant increase in nerve growth factor (NGF) activity, which has been reported to have chemotactic activity for neutrophils, and which can induce secretion of interleukin 1 (known to be an endogenous pyrogen), was detected in serum samples of febrile horses following long-distance transport (Kawamoto *et al.* 1996). These results suggest possible roles of neutrophilic cytokines, such as G-CSF and NGF, in the onset of clinical manifestations such as pyrexia and the development of pneumonic lesions.

In summary, the results described above suggest that the classical clinical signs of shipping fever might be largely caused by the development of pneumonic lesions during road transport. These may be associated with opportunistic infection by resident bacteria, *i.e.*, *Streptococcus equi* subsp. *zooepidemicus*.

Pathogenesis of pneumonia in horses experimentally infected with *Streptococcus equi* subspecies *zooepidemicus*

In order to evaluate the possibility that *Strep. z.* is the causative bacterial agent of equine pneumonia associated with transport, as well as to investigate its pathogenesis, 10 horses were experimentally infected with *Strep. z.* and pathological examinations were carried out (unpublished data, JRA). Seven Thoroughbreds and three Anglo-Arabian horses, ranging from 2-4 yr in age, were inoculated, via an endoscope, into the caudodorsal region of the left caudal lung lobe with a dose of 30 ml of $1{\sim}7{\times}10^8$ CFU/ml of *Strep. z.* After inoculation, necropsy and microscopic examinations were sequentially conducted 30 min, 1, 2, 3, 4, 17, 20 h and 2 wk later.

The results of the intrapulmonary innoculation of *Strep. z.* are as follows:

(1) Experimentally-induced pneumonia was characterized by serous hemorrhagic pneumonia, by hemorrhagic purulent pneumonia, as well as by purulent coagulative necrotic pneumonia, depending on the time course.

(2) The bacteria were isolated from mucus, serous fluid, and pulmonary effusions; these fluids were characterized cytologically by inflammatory changes. Further, the bacteria showed resistance against phagocytosis by pulmonary alveolar macrophages (PAM) and neutrophils. Lymphocyte reaction was slight or lacking. Thus, the inhibition of neutrophil and PAM function are considered to be important in the development of pneumonia.

When pathogenic micoorganisms invade, the acute inflammatory reaction that centers around the neutrophilic infiltration occurs first, and the migration and aggregation of monocytes and macrophages to the local site occurs afterward. When the activating macrophage engulfs pathogenic microorganisms, various cytokines are produced. Because neutrophils and macrophages at the sites of focal pneumonia in these cases were greatly degenerated and collapsed, and bacteria survived in these cells, we considered that the function of these cells was compromised. This suggests that *Strep. z.* has resistance to PAM and neutrophils. The existence of a protective M-like protein that has acid resistance, heat resistance, or anti-phagocytotic function has been identified on the surface of *Strep. z.* Determining the tissue injury properties of the protective M-like protein, as well as its pathogenicity (antiphagocytic function), remain problems to be studied in the future. Preliminary evidence suggests these properties may be related to the hyaluronic acid capsule of *Strep z.* and to leucocidin secreted from *Strep. z.* (*unpublished data*). Based on the profuse migration of neutrophils to the infected tissue, it is likely that there is a neutrophil chemotactic factor or substance (like the protective M-like protein) that *Strep. z.* possesses, or these effects may be due to leukotoxin.

(3) With the progression of the disease, the neutrophils often adhered to the endothelial surface of the alveolar capillary lumen and played a role in generating coagulation necrosis of lung tissues.

(4) Pleuritis was noted in close relation to interlobular septal exudative inflammation.

From the above findings, the histopathological characteristics of experimented infection by *Strep. z.* closely resemble those of naturally occuring equine pneumonia associated with transport. There is strong evidence that *Strep. z.* is implicated as a causal factor in transport-related respiratory disease.

■ Predisposing factors for equine respiratory

Although transport of bovids is known to impair *in vitro* function of bovine alveolar macrophages and transit-associated stress is thought to be a predisposing factor in the development of transport-related respiratory and enteric diseases in these species, there have been few studies examining the effects of road transport on the responses of equine pulmonary defense mechanisms (Anderson *et al.* 1985, Bayly *et al.* 1986, O'Callaghan *et al.* 1987, Traub-Dargatz *et al.* 1988, Leadon 1989, Crisman *et al.* 1992, Smith *et al.* 1996a, Hobo *et al.* 1997, Raidal *et al.* 1997). Crisman *et al.* (1992) reported the effects of road transport on constituents of BALF from seven healthy Thoroughbreds shipped 1,160 km over 36 h. They concluded that the phagocyctic activity of PAM collected in the BALF was not altered by the transport. Traub-Dargatz *et al.* (1988) also reported that there was no increased response of phagocytic function of PAM collected from BALF from horses immediately following transport, although they observed changes 5 d following road transport. They concluded that the delayed inflammatory response was the result of the transport stress. In contrast, alveolar macrophage numbers and activity in recently transported horses with influenza were significantly reduced one week after transport in another study. (Anderson *et al.* 1985.)

Hobo *et al.* studied the effects of 41 h of road transportation on the composition of BALF obtained from 30 Thoroughbreds with no histo-

Early diagnosis of respiratory disease using ELISA for surfactant proteins

Classical signs of shipping fever, such as pyrexia, depression, soft cough, and shallow frequent respirations, may reflect the presence of acute pneumonia that occurs during transport (Oikawa *et al.* 1995). It has been proposed that hematological and biochemical parameters such as peripheral leucocyte and neutrophil counts and fibrinogen concentration might be used to indicate inflammatory changes in horses affected with shipping fever. However, clinical signs and changes in these biochemical parameters are not pathognomonic for pneumonia. No hematological and biochemical markers have yet been established that are specific for shipping fever pneumonia. Thus, evaluating the presence and severity of pneumonic lesions associated with transport by using a simple method may be of value clinically as an aide to early diagnosis and to establishing the prognosis for sick horses.

Pulmonary surfactant is synthesized and secreted by alveolar type II cells into the fluid layer that covers the alveolar epithelium. The surfactant spreads at the air-liquid interface and, by decreasing surface tension, protects the alveoli against collapse at the end of expiration. In addition, pulmonary surfactant may play an important role in the host's pulmonary defenses. The major components of surfactant are phospholipids. There are four distinct surfactant-specific proteins, designated surfactant protein-A (SP-A), surfactant protein-B (SP-B), surfactant protein-C (SP-C) and surfactant protein-D (SP-D).

Our group has recently prepared monoclonal antibodies against equine SP-A and SP-D and developed enzyme-linked immunosorbent (ELISA) assays for them (Hobo *et al.* 1999a, 1999b, 1999c, 1999d). In a series of studies, we determined the concentrations of SP-A and SP-D in BALF and sera of 20 horses while they were being transported for 41 h (Hobo *et al.* 1999c, 1999d). We found that phosphatidylglycerol, SP-A and SP-D concentrations in BALF collected after transport were significantly decreased relative to pre-transport concentrations, suggesting a reduction in the quantity of surfactant (Hobo *et al.* 1999c, 1999d). Neutrophil counts, total protein and albumin concentrations in BALF were significantly increased in 6 horses with pyrexia out of 20 transported horses. Additionally, the maximum serum SP-A concentration or the concentration of SP-A in serum 5 hours before the onset of pyrexia (fever) increased significantly in the 6 febrile horses (Hobo *et al.* 1999e). We speculate that this phenomenon results from increased leakage of SP-A into the blood as a result of injury at the alveolar-capillary barrier due to bacterial infection (Hobo *et al.* 1999e). We are optimistic that this approach might serve as a foundation for future studies of clinical evaluation of surfactant proteins in sera. This approach has great promise as a clinical marker for transport-associated respiratory disease, both to predict the onset of the disease and to evaluate its severity.

AREAS FOR FUTURE STUDY

(1) To determine the biological effects of vibration and jolting on horses with and without previous transport experience. Additionally, to determine what frequencies of vibration or oscillation are associated with deleterious biological effects in horses. These findings could be used to develop road transport vehicles with vibration characteristics that produce minimal adverse effects in horses.

(2) To clarify the causes and mechanisms of lower respiratory tract bacterial contamination associated with road transport. Particularly important is to clarify the effect of head posture on airway clearance of contaminants or native bacteria.

(3) To clarify the relationships between length of journey (traveling time) and post-transport recovery period, particularly with respect to determining the interval of recovery required between transport episodes to minimize the incidence of transport-associated respiratory disease.

(4) To develop an easily identifiable and rapid diagnostic test for transport-associated respiratory disease, especially subclinical cases that are not readily recognized.

To further these aims, consideration should be given to the development and construction of a computer-controlled transport simulator. Such a device could be used to mimic the ride characteristics and environment of nearly any type of transport vehicle, and would enable experiments to be conducted on transport stress with minimal variation between runs due to differences in season, weather, traffic, etc.

In conclusion, there is substantial evidence that both the *quantity* (time) and *quality* (environmental and management factors) of the transport experience play a role in eliciting transport-associated disease in horses. Many horses travel regularly with few detectable adverse effects, so it is clearly possible for some horses to adapt to the demands of transport while remaining disease-free. The multitude of factors that potentially contribute to the development of transport-associated disease sug-

▪ Introduction

Fatality, injury, and disease are among the parameters that can be used to assess the degree of stress that occurs during farm animal transport.[1] However, more subtle measures may be required in the assessment of transit stress in horses. Stress in this context may occur where an abnormal or extreme adjustment in physiology or behavior is required to cope with the adverse effects of environment or management.[2]

Adverse changes in environment can be assessed in terms of temperature, relative humidity, and other factors. These potential sources of stress were quantified during a flight that carried 112 horses from London, England to Sydney, Australia. A series of blood samples were collected to assess their usefulness in the post-transit assessment of normal horses and those affected by "shipping fever."

▪ Materials & Methods

Airplane and Flight Details: A Boeing 747 F freighter used exclusively for charter flights carried 25 freight pallets on which wooden horse stalls were placed so as to leave a single access aisle on the right of the aircraft. Each pallet could accommodate five horses in individual stalls. The flight engineer selected the maximum flow rate of 2,500 cu ft air/minute for ventilation of the cargo hold for the entire duration of the flight and selected a temperature of +18 C for this area of the plane. The cruising altitude was 35,000 ft, and the cargo area was pressurized to an altitude equivalent to 8,000 ft. Three refueling and/or loading and unloading stops were planned for the journey, which had an estimated duration of 37 hours.

Horses: A total of 112 horses were carried on this flight. They were of various breeds, ages and sexes, and their body weights ranged from 350 to 500 kg. Each had entered a preflight quarantine station 4 weeks prior to departure for Australia, and each re-entered quarantine for 2 weeks after the completion of their journey. A clinical examination was carried out prior to departure and on arrival, and thereafter as required.

Environmental Studies: Wet and dry bulb thermometers[a] were placed on the side section of eight of the horse stalls. These thermometers were placed in the rear (three), mid (two), and forward (three) sections of the plane and at a level that approximated the nostril height of the horses. The wet and dry bulb temperature and relative humidity were recorded from each thermometer at 1- to 4-hour intervals from the initial take off to the final landing while the aircraft was in flight, and every hour during refueling or technical stops. A hand-held battery-operated centrifugal air sampler[b] was used to identify and quantify the colony forming units present in the air in the rear, mid, and forward sections of the main cargo area. Air samples were again taken at a level that approximated the nostril height of the horses, at a position to the rear of the horses' heads to avoid unnecessary contamination from the breath of the horses. This sampler was used to discharge the colony forming units in samples of 20 liters of air on to agarose[c] and Rose-Bengal containing agarose[d] strips. Air samples were taken in the cargo hold at intervals similar to those used for recording air temperature and relative humidity. All strips were sealed immediately on completion of sampling, and all were incubated either during the journey or on arrival until clear visualization of colonies was achieved.

Hematology and Blood Chemistry: Blood samples were collected from the jugular vein while the horses were in the quarantine station in England on the morning of departure and within 1 hour of arrival at their destination in the quarantine station in Australia. Although all horses appeared normal on arrival, signs of respiratory disease were noted on either the first or second day after arrival in seven individuals. Blood samples were collected from normal horses (n=20) and those with respiratory disease (n=7) on arrival, at 12 hours, on Days 1,2,3,7,and 14 thereafter. Samples for hematology were kept at +4 C until counted within 24 hours of collection. Serum and plasma samples were separated within 6 hours of collection and held at -18 C until assayed within 3 days of collection. White blood cells were counted with a single channel Coulter Counter[e] and the differential count was carried out on Diff-Quik[f] stained smears using the battlement method of counting. Total protein was measured by a modification of the Biuret method[3] and albumen levels by a modification of the bromocresol green method using a Cobas Mira Discrete Analyzer[g]. Globulin levels were recorded as the difference between the total protein and serum albumen levels. Plasma fibrinogen levels were measured with an automated modification of Clauss method[4,h].

Statistical tests: A Students "t" test was used in the data comparisons in this study.

■ Results

Airplane and Flight Details: No technical difficulties were encountered during this flight which proceeded as planned and had an actual total duration of 39 hours rather than the planned 37 hours. The flight durations between refueling and/or technical stops were sequentially 7,7,6, and 4 hours from the initial take off to the final landing. The sta-

Table I. *Comparison of temperature and relative humidity values recorded in the main cargo hold of a Boeing 747 F carrying 112 horses from England to Australia when the plane was stationary and when it was in flight.*

Status	Temperature (C) n=128 Mean ±SD	Range	Relative Humidity (%) n=128 Mean ±SD	Range
Stationary	20.7 ± 3.4	11 - 27	71.2 ± 9.1	45 - 91
In flight	17.9 ± 2.7*	10 - 27	37.8 ± 0.6*	23 - 75

*$p<0.001$

tionary periods at intermediate stopping points were sequentially, 9, 2, and 4 hours.

Horses: No fatalities occurred among the horses during travel or during the post-transit quarantine period. Seven horses demonstrated signs of "shipping fever" after arrival, but each made a satisfactory recovery in response to medical treatment.

Environmental Studies: Air temperature and relative humidity values recorded in the main cargo hold while the plane was in flight and during the stationary periods resulting from refueling or loading and unloading are summarized in Table I. A temperature and relative humidity gradient was observed to be present from the front of the plane to the rear during flight and while the plane was stationary (Table II). The difference in the mean temperatures between the front and rear was greater (+12 C) while the aircraft was stationary than when it was in flight (+3 C). The relative humidity was observed to exceed 90% at the rear of the aircraft during refueling and unloading.

Mean ± SD counts of colony forming units per 20 liters of air recorded in the main cargo hold at various stages of each flight and while the plane was stationary are summarized in Table III. The mean (±SD) colony forming unit counts for bacteria recorded while the aircraft was stationary (1,486 ± 713), were significantly different ($p<0.001$) from those recorded while the aircraft was in flight (326 ± 242). The decline in CFU counts from the higher values present during stationary periods was progressive during the subsequent inflight periods. Fungal counts were also elevated at some stages of the journey, but the differences between fungal counts during stationary and in flight periods were not significant.

The total white blood cell (WBC) counts in horses affected by shipping fever were significantly higher ($p<0.05$) than those obtained from the normal horses on the second day after arrival even though they were within the normal range of preflight values (Table IV). Values for WBC counts in horses with shipping fever exceeded this range thereafter.

Table II. *Comparison of temperature and relative humidity values obtained at the front and rear sections of a Boeing 747 F freighter carrying 112 horses from England to Australia while stationary and in flight.*

Status	Mean Temperature (C) n=32 Front	Rear	Mean Relative Humidity (%) n=32 Front	Rear
Stationary	21	33	78	91
In flight	13*	16*	25*	41*

*p<0.05

Table III. *Counts of colony forming units (CFU) per 20 liters of air recorded in the main cargo hold of a Boeing 747 F carrying 112 horses from England to Australia while the plane was stationary and in flight.*

Stage of Journey	Mean CFU/20 l Air ± SD Bacteria	Fungi
Initial loading	130 ± 132	132 ± 68
Flight No.1		
Take off	130 ± 41	84 ± 29
+ 1hr	69 ± 4	30 ± 2
+ 4hr	78 ± 56	22 ± 15
+ 7hr	174 ± 200	312 ± 225
Stationary Period 1		
+ 9hrs	2522 ± 2474	331 ± 80
Flight No. 2		
+ 4hrs	689 ± 333	631 ± 613
+ 7hrs	473 ± 146	217 ± 180
Stationary Period 2		
+2hrs	1395 ± 550	880 ± 486
Flight No. 3		
+2hrs	655 ± 405	570 ± 625
+6hrs	235 ± 78	231 ± 38
Stationary Period 3		
+4hrs	983 ± 305	278 ± 92
Flight No. 4		
+3 hrs	433 ± 290	342 ± 65
Final Unloading	1046 ± 281	202 ± 83

Neutrophil counts in normal horses on arrival were markedly and significantly ($p<0.001$) different from preflight counts (Table V). Neutrophil counts in horses with shipping fever were significantly greater than those in normal horses on Days 2, 7, and 14. This pattern was similar to that seen in comparisons of WBC counts except that neutrophil counts in horses affected by shipping fever on the second day after arrival exceeded the range present in normal horses prior to departure.

Globulin elevations were not noted in horses with shipping fever until some days had elapsed after arrival (Table VI). There were, however, significant elevations in fibrinogen on Day 1 in normal horses ($p<0.001$) and even greater elevations ($p<0.05$) in the horses with shipping fever (Table VII) from Day 2 onward.

Table IV. *Comparison of the numbers of white blood cells (WBCs) in normal horses and those affected by shipping fever.*

	Mean WBC ± SD (x10^9/l)	
	Normal Horses n=20	Horses with Shipping Fever n=7
Prior to flight	9.7 ± 1.9	--
On arrival	10.4 ± 2.4	--
12 h	9.2 ± 1.6	--
Day 1	7.6 ± 1.3	--
Day 2	6.4 ± 1.1	*8.2 ± 0.3
Day 3	--	--
Day 7	8.3 ± 1.9	*12.7 ± 1.6
Day 14	8.7 ± 1.9	*11.8 ± 1.7

*p<0.05

■ Discussion

The environments experienced by these 112 horses during this long distance flight differed significantly during the in-flight and stationary sections of the journey (Table I). In all modern jet planes, air flows from the front to the rear during flight. Cold atmospheric air of low relative humidity enters the ventilation system at altitude and, although the system warms the air, it tends to create a cooler drier environment in the front of the plane and a warmer more moist environment at the rear (Table II). These differences may not be of much practical importance as the "comfort zone" of 25 C and 80% relative humidity was exceeded only for short periods, and the horses should have been capable of accommodating this potential stressor. However, the counts of colony forming units (Table III) illustrate that the challenge to the mucociliary system of the respiratory tract during stationary periods can be considerable. Air clearance rates within the cargo hold during stationary periods are reduced to a level considerably below the 2,500 cu ft air/minute that is attained at altitude. These rates are not quantifiable with the instruments available to the flight engineer. The surges in colony forming unit counts that occur take at least several hours to

Table V. *Comparison of mean neutrophil counts (1) prior to flight and after flight in normal horses and (2) after flight between normal horses and horses with shipping fever.*

	Mean Neutrophils ± SD (x 10^9/l)	
	Normal Horses n=20	Horses with Shipping Fever n=7
Prior to flight	4.1 ± 0.5	--
On arrival	**8.4 ± 2.3	--
12 h	6.9 ± 1.8	--
Day 1	5.0 ± 1.3	--
Day 2	3.6 ± 0.9	*5.8 ± 0.6
Day 3	--	--
Day 7	5.9 ± 1.4	**9.2 ± 0.9
Day 14	5.4 ± 1.5	*7.9 ± 1.2

**p<0.001
*p<0.05

Table VI. *Comparison of the mean changes in globulin in normal horses and those affected by shipping fever.*

	Mean Globulin ± SD (g/l)	
	Normal Horses n=20	Horses with Shipping Fever n=7
Prior to flight	27.5 ± 3.8	--
On arrival	29.1 ± 2.7	--
12 h	29.4 ± 2.7	--
Day 1	30.0 ± 3.5	--
Day 2	27.6 ± 3.5	28.1 ± 0.8
Day 3	29.9 ± 3.8	--
Day 7	29.3 ± 3.5	**41.5 ± 2.5
Day 14	29.6 ± 3.6	*37.3 ± 5.3

*p<0.05
**p<0.001

Table VII. *Comparison of mean fibrinogen levels prior to flight and after flight in normal horses and after flight between normal horses and horses with shipping fever.*

	Mean Fibrinogen ± SD (g/l)	
	Normal Horses n=20	Horses with Shipping Fever n=7
Prior to flight	1.6 ± 0.2	--
On arrival	--	--
12 h	--	--
Day 1	**2.8 ± 0.5	--
Day 2	2.5 ± 0.7	*3.2 ± 0.2
Day 3	2.4 ± 0.5	--
Day 7	2.0 ± 0.5	*3.1 ± 0.4
Day 14	1.7 ± 0.5	2.2 ± 0.3

**p<0.001
*p<0.05

be reduced to the low levels seen in the initial stages of flight. The combination of the effects of changes in temperature and relative humidity coupled with changes in colony forming unit counts may be a factor that contributes to the development of post-transit shipping fever, and this could be a rewarding area for further study.

There were significant postflight elevations in neutrophil counts and fibrinogen levles in the apparently normal horses. These changes may reflect otherwise inapparent responses to confinement and transport or, perhaps too, the initial signs of subclinical and otherwise undetected respiratory disease. This is another area that could benefit from further research. Seven of the 112 horses (6.3%) that traveled on this flight manifested evidence of shipping fever/respiratory disease, on either Day 1 or Day 2 after arrival. Each horse with shipping fever made a good recovery from illness following broad-spectrum antimicrobial and supportive therapy. The horses with respiratory disease had significantly elevated white blood cell and neutrophil counts with elevated globulin and fibrinogen in the post-transit quarantine period despite intensive therapy and monitoring.

The results suggest that horses with shipping fever occurring in association with long distance journeys by air may have neutrophil counts > 5.8 x 10/1 and fibrinogen levels > 3.2 g/1. This information when taken into account in the context of a clinical examination may assist clinicians in the diagnosis of shipping fever prior to the emergence of the full clinical syndrome on Days 1 or 2 after a long air journey.

---

1. Halls MR. *Transport stress in animals - a review.* Anim Reg Stud 1978;1:289-343.
2. Fraser D, Ritchie JSD, Fraser AF. *The term "stress" in a verterinary context.* Br Vet J 1975;131:653-662.
3. Kingsley EG. *The direct Biuret method for the determination of serum protein as applied to photometric and visual colorimetry.* J. Lab Clin Med 1942;27:840.
4. Clauss A. *Ger inungsphysiologische Schneilmethode zur bestimmung des fibrionogens.* Acta Haematolog 1957;17:237-246.

---

a. Brannon, London, England.
b. Biotest, Frankfurt, West Germany.
c. Agar Strip GKA, Biotest, Frankfurt, West Germany.
d. Agar Strip, HS, Biotest, Frankfurt, West Germany.
e. Coulter Model ZF, B.M. Browne, Stillorgan, Dublin, Ireland.
f. Diff-Quik Merz and Dade B.M. Browne, Stillorgan, Dublin, Ireland.
g. Cobas Mira Discrete Analyzer, Roche, B.M. Browne, Stillorgan, Dublin, Ireland.
h. Coagulometer, B.M. Browne, Stillorgan, Dublin, Ireland.

BODY WEIGHT, RECTAL TEMPERATURE, HAEMATOLOGY AND BLOOD BIOCHEMISTRY prior to transport and for three days after arrival, in racehorses transported by air to international races in Hong Kong

D.P. Leadon, MA, MVB, MSc, FRCVS and K. Watkins, BVSc, MRCVS

■ Summary

Body weight, rectal temperature, haematology and blood biochemistry parameters were studied in 18 Thoroughbred racehorses that were transported from overseas to compete in the Hong Kong Invitational Bowl and Cup in December 1993. Mean bodyweight fell from 496.8 to 478.9 kgs. And mean pre-flight weights were not regained by Day 3 after arrival. A mild pyrexia (101.0 F) was evident on arrival and although horses that had an uneventful journey were no longer febrile by Day 1, horses that had a difficult journey remained febrile until Day 2. Plasma cortisol was elevated from pre flight (5.2 ± 2.3 pg/ul) to arrival (7.9 ± 2.1 pg/ul). PMNL's ($60.6 \pm 6.7\%$) and lymphocytes ($35.1 \pm 4.2\%$) were also significantly different prior to departure, ($72.1 \pm 5.3\%$) and ($20.5 \pm 7.1\%$) respectively, than on arrival. Significant differences were seen in PCV (43.9 ± 5.5 to 47.5 ± 3.8 1/l) and plasma albumin (32.3 ± 1.7 to 33.8 ± 1.4 g/l) in all horses on arrival and also on Day 1. Plasma chloride (100.8 ± 2.8 to 102.7 ± 2.1 meq/l) changes were only present on arrival, in horses that had a difficult journey. Changes also occurred in plasma bilirubin (T) (49.6 ± 15.7 to 81.8 ± 25.1 mmol/l) and AST (202.3 ± 85.2 to 237.8 ± 67.9 iu/l), but these again were only present on Day 1 after arrival. Plasma fibrinogen concentration (1.05 ± 0.2 to 1.2 ± 0.3 g/l) did not return to pre flight levels by Day 3 after arrival. None of the parameters examined in this study relate directly to performance. The present study suggests that normal horses should be allowed at least three days to recover from the effects of transport, prior to racing after long air journeys.

Reprinted with permission of R & W Publications (Newmarket) Limited., Suites 3 & 4, 8 Kings Court, Willie Snaith Road, Newmarket, Suffolk, CB8 7SG UK, e-mail address: <rw.publications@btinterntet.com>

Introduction

Horse racing authorities in many countries are encouraging international participation in invitational races (*e.g.* the Breeders Cup series in the USA, the Japan Cup in Tokyo, the Rothmans International in Canada and the Hong Kong Cup and Bowl). Appropriate/optimal recovery periods which should be provided after long distance air transport are the subject of current debate within the racing industry. There are trainers who advocate sending horses to other countries on the day before racing and others who prefer to travel a week or more in advance of the event. There are at present, no scientific evidence on which to base guidance on appropriate recovery periods, prior to competition in races and similar equestrian events.

Horses transported by air will be exposed to changes in temperature, relative humidity and the numbers of micro-organisms within the inhaled air (Leadon *et al.* 1990). These factors and other potential stressors are associated with significant post transport elevations in mean polymorphonuclear leucocytes (PMNL) counts and fibrinogen levels even in apparently normal horses after long haul flights (Leadon *et al.* 1990). The previous report, which described a mixed population of various breeds of horses, none of which were intended to race within weeks after arrival, is the only study of it's type. There are no published studies of the rate of return to pre-flight values for any parameters in a group of racehorses intended for racing within a few days of a long distance air transport.

The present study describes changes in clinical and laboratory parameters in racehorses transported by air to a major international racing festival. It provides guidance for clinicians and racing authorities on appropriate recovery periods, prior to resumed maximal exercise or racing. This information is also a source of reference for future studies.

Materials & Methods

Horses: A total of 18 Thoroughbred racehorses that had been invited to compete in the Hong Kong Invitational Bowl and Cup in December 1993 were included in the study. Three groups were formed retrospectively; Group I (total group n=18) later divided into two sub-groups viz; Group Ia (uneventful journey to Hong Kong in which rest stops occurred as scheduled, n=9) Group Ib (journey interrupted by adverse weather or technical delays with unscheduled stops, n=9). An additional 10 Thoroughbred racehorses in training, based in Hong Kong, were used as non-transported controls (Group II) for endocrine studies.

Transport: Group I horses were transported by road from their stables in either Australia, France, New Zealand, Singapore, the UK or the USA to the nearest international airport. They traveled by air in "jet stalls"/air-stables capable of carrying a maximum of three horses to Hong Kong. They were offered water every six hours and hay ad lib throughout the air journey and the transfer time from arrival at Hong Kong airport to the racecourse stables was 1 hour. Total journey times varied in each sub-group (Group 1a; 6 - 36 hours and Group Ib 12 - 39 hours). The interval between arrival and racing ranged from 3 to 9 days.

Body Weight: Body weight was recorded by the trainer or clinician prior to departure and by the authors on arrival in Hong Kong at the racecourse quarantine stables and each of the three following mornings.

Rectal Temperature: Rectal temperature was recorded on arrival, and on each of the next three mornings (Group I).

Blood Samples: Jugular venous blood samples were collected prior to departure, on arrival and each of the next three mornings (Group I). Similar samples were collected morning and afternoon for three successive days (Group I). It was not possible, for logistical reasons, to obtain all scheduled samples from all horses.

PCV and white cell estimations were carried out by practice or referral laboratories in the countries of origin prior to departure and in the laboratories of the Royal Hong Kong Jockey Club, using an Abbot Cell-Dyn analyser on arrival and thereafter. Clinicians in each of the countries of origin of Group I horses forwarded separated, frozen heparinised blood samples collected on the morning prior to transport, in insulated containers with the horses to Hong Kong. These samples were thawed at 4 C on arrival.

Blood biochemical assays (Total protein, albumin, bilirubin (T), CK and AST) were carried out at 30 C within 12 hrs of receipt, using a Cobas Mira-S analyser. Sodium, potassium and chloride were measured using a Corning 435 flame photometer. Plasma fibrinogen concentrations were measured with an automated modification of the Clauss method (Clauss 1957).

Cortisol assays (Cortisol Coat-A-Count, Diagnostics Corporation, Los Angeles, CA 90045, USA) were performed later on samples that had been stored at -18 C using a Beckman Gamma 5500 Radiation Counter (Beckman Corp., Fullerton, CA 92634, USA).

■ Statistics

Data was entered into a spreadsheet software programme (Excel 4, Microsoft Corporation, Redmond, WA, USA) and analysed using Sutdent's "T" test in a statistical software package (Data Desk 4, Data Description Inc., Ithaca, NY, USA) on an Apple Macintosh IIsi computer. Differences that were statistically significant were identified by superscripts.

■ Results

Horses: All the grooms that accompanied these horses considered them to have traveled well. One horse was found to have pleuro-pneumonia on clinical examination on arrival.

Body Weight: Bodyweights recorded on arrival were significantly lower ($p<0.005$) than those recorded in the countries of origin (Table I). Weight was gained over the following three days. The majority of the weight gain occurred between arrival and the first subsequent day. Horses had not returned to their pre transport bodyweight by the third day.

Rectal Temperature: Rectal temperatures were elevated on arrival (Table 2). They declined by either the following morning (Group Ia) or by the second morning (Group Ib).

Blood Samples: Plasma cortisol concentrations were higher on arrival than on departure in Group Ib, and they were higher on arrival than on either Day 2 or Day 3 in Group I (Table 3).

WBC did not differ significantly, but PMNL and lymphocyte % obtained on arrival were significantly higher and lower respectively, ($p<0.005$) than those recorded in the countries of origin (Table 4).

PCV, plasma albumin (Table 5) and chloride (Table 6) were significantly increased when pre-departure samples were compared with those obtained on arrival.

Bilirubin (T) concentrations were also significantly elevated on arrival and they did not return to pre-transport levels until after the second morning (Table 7).

Plasma fibrinogen concentrations increased between arrival and the first morning and they were higher in Group Ib than in Group Ia on the third morning (Table 8).

Plasma CK was not significantly altered by transport but AST values were higher on arrival than on departure and they did not decline until the third morning (Table 9). Two horses were excluded from analysis of muscle enzyme data as a result of minor muscle injuries which were not sustained during transport.

■ Discussion

The racehorses that were transported (Group I) lost approximately 20 kgs bodyweight in the course of their journeys to Hong Kong. This represented only 4% of their bodyweight (Table I). Faecal lossed may be important in transport related weight loss in cattle, where the total loss is primarily due to evacuation of bowel contents (Tarrant 1990). This was not the case with these horses as they were given hay throughout the journey.

There is no clear explanation for the febrile response seen in all horses on arrival (Table 2). All horses, even those that are clinically normal, may have a low grade inflammatory response as a consequence of the "head held high" posture that results from tying of head collars to stallfixings and confinement in stalls in aircraft (Tackyleft and Love 1990).

The higher plasma cortisol concentrations present on the first morning after arrival in Hong Kong (Table 3) may reflect either the stress of the journey or the stress associated with being in an unfamiliar environment. Standardization of methodology for WBC ($x10^9/l$), PMNL

Table 1. Bodyweight (Kgs, $\bar{x} \pm$ s.d.) pre-transport, on arrival and on the following three mornings.

	PRE	ARRIVAL	DAY 1	DAY 2	DAY 3	P
Group I	496.8[a] ±36.9 n=10	478.9[b] ±37.4 n=18	483.8 ±38.3 n=17	483.4 ±40.4 n=17	485.3[c] ±40.3 n=16	ab p<=0.005 bd p<=0.005 ac p<=0.05
Group Ia	499.8 ±48.6 n=5	477.2[d] ±47.1 n=9	480.2 ±47.1 n=9	482.3 ±47.1 n=9	482.6[e] ±47.1 n=9	de p<=0.05
Group Ib	493.8[f] ±25.9 n=5	480.5[g] ±27.3 n=9	487.8[h] ±27.7 n=8	484.5 ±29.3 n=8	488.6[i] ±29.9 n=7	fi p<=0.008 gh p<=0.05

Table 2. *Rectal Temperature (F, $\bar{x} \pm$ s.d.) on arrival and on the following three mornings.*

	ARRIVAL	DAY 1	DAY 2	DAY 3	P
Group I	101.0[a] ±0.47 n=18	100.3[b] ±0.7 n=18	100.1 ±0.4 n=16	100.2 ±0.4 n=13	ab p<=0.0008
Group Ia	101.1[c] ±0.5 n=9	100.2[d] ±0.4 n=9	100.2 ±0.4 n=9	100.2 ±0.4 n=9	cd p<=0.0005
Group Ib	101.0[e] ±0.2 n=9	100.5 ±0.9 n=8	100.0[f] ±0.5 n=8	100.2 ±0.5 n=8	ef p<=0.0003

Table 3. *Plasma cortisol (pg/ul), ($\bar{x} \pm$ s.d.) Group I - pre-transport, on arrival and on the following three mornings and Group II - on three successive mornings and afternoons.*

	PRE	ARRIVAL	DAY 1	DAY 2	DAY 3	P
Group I	5.2 ±2.3 n=9	7.9[a] ±2.1 n=18	7.0 ±1.6 n=18	6.1[b] ±1.5 n=17	6.4[c] ±1.5 n=17	ab p<=0.005 ac p<=0.005
Group Ia	6.7 ±1.6 n=4	8.3 ±1.5 n=9	7.0 ±1.8 n=8	6.2 ±1.5 n=9	6.7 ±1.6 n=8	
Group Ib	4.0[d] ±2.1 n=5	7.5e ±2.6 n=9	6.9 ±1.6 n=9	5.9 ±1.6 n=8	6.0 ±1.6 n=8	de p<=0.01
Group II am			5.1[f] ±1.9 n=10	6.3[h] ±1.6 n=10	5.6[k] ±3.4 n=10	fg p<=0.05 fh p<=0.05 hi p<=0.05
Group II pm			3.4[g] ±0.8 n=10	4.1[i] ±1.8 n=10	3.1[l] ±1.3 n=10	ki p<=0.05

and Lymphocyte % was not possible because of the multi-national nature of this study. However, PMNL and Lymphocyte % (Table 4) were similar on Day 3 to pre-departure and this would seem to suggest that the changes seen in these parameters gave at least a general impression of the actual responses to travel. Changes in plasma cortisol, PMNL and lymphocytes were transient and no longer evident by Day 3 after arrival. The values obtained for these parameters suggest that the degree of stress associated with transport was of a low order of magnitude.

Table 4. WBC (x10⁹/1), PMNL and lymphocytes (%) ($\bar{x} \pm$ s.d.) pre-transport, on arrival and on the following three mornings.

	PRE	ARRIVAL	DAY 1	DAY 2	DAY 3	P
WBC Group I	8.0 ±2.5 n=12	8.0 ±1.5 n=18	10.2 ±2.4 n=18	8.7 ±3.0 n=14	8.7 ±2.0 n=11	
WBC Group Ia	8.8 ±3.7 n=6	8.6 ±1.6 n=9	10.1 ±2.1 n=9	8.6 ±1.2 n=9	8.5 ±1.4 n=9	
WBC Group Ib	7.4 ±1.2 n=6	7.4 ±1.3 n=9	10.5 ±2.8 n=9	8.9 ±5.2 n=5	10.0 n=2	
PMNL Group I	60.6ª ±6.7 n=9	72.1ᵇ ±5.3 n=17	65.7 ±9.5 n=18	63.2 ±8.6 n=14	60.8 ±6.9 n=11	ab $p \leq 0.005$
PMNL Group Ia	57 ±8.0 n=4	72.6 ±6.2 n=9	63.9 ±8.8 n=9	59.7 ±6.0 n=9	58.4 ±4.1 n=9	
PMNL Group Ib	63.4 ±4.4 n=5	71.4 ±4.4 n=8	67.6 ±10.4 n=9	69.7 ±9.2 n=5	71.7 n=2	
Lymphs Group I	35.1ª ±4.2 n=8	20.5ᵇ ±7.1 n=17	27.0 ±9.4 n=18	29.6 ±7.8 n=14	30.3 ±6.2 n=11	ab $p \leq 0.001$
Lymphs Group Ia	35.3 ±5.5 n=3	21.0 ±5.8 n=9	28.3 ±8.1 n=9	33.0 ±5.4 n=9	32.5 ±4.1 n=9	
Lymphs Group Ib	35.0 ±3.9 n=5	19.9 ±8.8 n=8	25.8 ±10.8 n=9	23.7 ±8.5 n=5	20.7 n=2	

Although water loss as evidenced by increases in PCV and plasma albumin (Table 5) occurred from departure to arrival, this was not so severe as to have resulted in dehydration. Pre-flight levels of albumin were not regained by the conclusion of the study period on Day 3 after arrival in the delayed journey group, but the mean value was still within normal limits. Plasma chloride was the only electrolyte measured in which a change was seen from pre to post flight values (Table 6). This finding suggests that extensive electrolyte supplementation prior to flying may be unnecessary.

Although plasma bilirubin concentration was significantly elevated from departure to arrival (Table 7) perhaps reflecting an abnormally reduced dietary intake, the apparent downward trend seen over the following three days was not significantly different. Further studies with larger numbers of horses could show that bilirubin has a potentially useful role in monitoring recovery after transport.

Table 5. PCV (1.1) and plasma albumin (g/l), ($\bar{x} \pm$ s.d.) pre-transport, on arrival and on the following three mornings.

	PRE	ARRIVAL	DAY 1	DAY 2	DAY 3	P
PCV Group I	43.9[a] ±5.5 n=10	47.5[b] ±3.8 n=17	49.2[c] ±5.3 n=18	45.9 ±3.3 n=14	46.2 ±3.1 n=11	ab $p<=0.05$ ac $p<=0.002$
PCV Group Ia	47.2 ±4.2 n=5	47.0 ±4.0 n=9	49.1 ±5.3 n=9	46.4 ±3.2 n=9	46.5 ±3.2 n=2	
PCV Group Ib	44.8 ±3.4 n=5	48.1 ±3.7 n=8	49.3 ±5.6 n=9	45.1 ±3.8 n=5	44.8 ±3.4 n=2	
Albumin Group I	32.3[d] ±1.7 n=10	33.8 ±1.6 n=17	33.8[e] ±1.4 n=18	32.7 ±1.4 n=14	33.0[f] ±1.5 n=11	de $p<=0.05$ df $p<=0.05$
Albumin Group Ia	31.7 ±1.6 n=5	33.6 ±1.6 n=9	32.6 ±1.7 n=9	33.2 ±1.9 n=9	33.0 ±1.6 n=9	
Albumin Group Ib	33.0 ±1.7 n=5	34.3 ±1.2 n=8	34.0 ±1.2 n=9	33.0 ±0.7 n=5	33.0 ±1.4 n=2	

The significant elevation in plasma fibrinogen concentration from departure to arrival and the failure to regain pre flight levels by Day 3 after arrival (Table 8), may have been sequelae to the febrile response (Table 2). If so then the '"head held high" posture (Rackyleft and Love 1990) may cause more protracted periods of low grade inflammation than has previously been thought. The rate of recovery may be determined by the severity of the insult to the respiratory tract.

The AST elevation (Table 9) may reflect either the consequences of fast exercise in the final stage of preparation for the races prior to departure, or the effects of muscular work during the journey.

None of the parameters examined in this study relate directly to performance. In the current absence of any performance data, the present study seems to suggest that normal horses should be allowed at least three days to recover from the effects of transport, prior to racing after long air journeys.

Trainers must be made aware that not all horses are normal after long air journeys. One of the horses in this study developed shipping fever and 6% or more of horses that travel long distances by air will develop this condition (Leadon et al. 1990). It therefore seems advisable to plan to arrive seven days or more before racing, so that horses that

Table 6. Plasma sodium, potassium and chloride (meq/l) ($\bar{x} \pm s.d.$) pre-transport, on arrival and on the following three mornings.

	PRE	ARRIVAL	DAY 1	DAY 2	DAY 3	P
Na Group I	140.1 ±2.5 n=12	140.3 ±2.1 n=18	139.4 ±1.5 n=18	139.9 ±1.5 n=14	139.7 ±0.9 n=11	
Na Group Ia	139.8 ±1.8 n=6	140.6 ±2.2 n=9	139 ±1.3 n=9	139.8 ±1.1 n=9	139.7 ±1.0 n=9	
Na Group Ib	140.3 ±3.1 n=6	140.0 ±2.2 n=9	139.9 ±1.5 n=9	140 ±2.3 n=5	140 n=2	
K Group I	3.6 ±0.3 n=12	3.4 ±0.5 n=18	3.7 ±0.3 n=17	3.6 ±0.3 n=14	3.7 ±0.2 n=11	
K Group Ia	3.7 ±0.3 n=6	3.2 ±0.5 n=9	3.8 ±0.3 n=9	3.6 ±0.4 n=9	3.7 ±1.0 n=9	
K Group Ib	3.5 ±0.3 n=6	3.6 ±0.5 n=9	3.5 ±0.3 n=8	3.6 ±0.2 n=11	3.7 n=2	
Cl Group I	100.8[a] ±2.8 n=12	102.7[b] ±2.1 n=18	100.6 ±2.7 n=18	100.9 ±2.7 n=14	102.8 ±2.0 n=11	ab $p<=0.05$
Cl Group Ia	99.7 ±2.9 n=6	102.0 ±1.8 n=9	101.0 ±1.9 n=9	101.1 ±2.2 n=9	103.1 ±2.1 n=9	
Cl Group Ib	102.0 ±2.3 n=6	103.3 ±3.1 n=9	100.1 ±3.4 n=8	100.6 ±3.7 n=5	101.5 n=2	

Table 7. Plasma bilirubin (T) (mmol/l) ($\bar{x} \pm s.d.$) pre-transport, on arrival and on the following three mornings.

	PRE	ARRIVAL	DAY 1	DAY 2	DAY 3	P
Group I	49.6[a] ±15.7 n=11	81.8[b] ±25.1 n=18	68 ±18/6 n=18	64.4 ±18.2 n=14	54.8 ±11.6 n=11	ab $p<=0.0001$
Group Ia	50.5 ±16.3 n=6	80.0 ±24.1 n=9	69.0 ±17.8 n=9	61.2 ±14.6 n=9	55.4 ±12.7 n=9	
Group Ib	48.7 ±16.7 n=5	83.6 ±27.3 n=9	67.8 ±20.4 n=9	70.2 ±24.0 n=5	52.0 n=2	

Table 8. *Plasma fibrinogen concentration (g/l, $\bar{x} \pm$ s.d.) pre-transport, on arrival and on the following three mornings.*

	ARRIVAL	DAY 1	DAY 2	DAY 3	P
Group I	1.05[a] ±0.2 n=18	1.2[b] ±0.3 n=18	1.1 ±0.2 n=14	1.3 ±0.4 n=11	ab p<=0.05
Group Ia	1.0[c] ±0.2 n=9	1.2 ±0.3 n=9	1.2 ±0.2 n=9	1.2[d] ±0.3 n=9	cd p<=0.05
Group Ib	1.1 ±0.2 n=9	1.2 ±0.2 n=9	1.1 ±0.4 n=5	1.6 n=2	

Table 9. *Plasma CK and AST (iu/l), $\bar{x} \pm$ s.d.) pre-transport, on arrival and on the following three mornings.*

	PRE	ARRIVAL	DAY 1	DAY 2	DAY 3	P
CK Group I	87.5 ±66 n=12	49.1 ±14.2 n=18	139.3 ±257.6 n=16	75.0 ±88.9 n=13	53.3 ±31.1 n=11	
CK Group Ia	56.5 ±19.7 n=6	47.3 ±10.4 n=9	44.1 ±7.5 n=8	41.7 ±6.4 n=9	56.8 ±33.3 n=9	
CK Group Ib	18.8 ±84 n=6	150.8 ±17.7 n=9	60.0 ±24.1 n=8	80.8 ±71.9 n=4	37.5	
AST Group I	202.3[a] ±85.2 n=12	237.8[b] ±67.9 n=18	243.6 ±79.3 n=18	230.7 ±103.5 n=14	192.0 ±52.4 n=11	ab p<=0.05
AST Group Ia	161.3 ±66.1 n=6	223.8 ±55.1 n=9	220.9 ±46.0 n=9	201.4 ±42.3 n=9	201.4 ±53.6 n=9	
AST Group Ib	243.2 ±87.3 n=6	251.8 ±79.7 n=9	266.2 ±100.5 n=9	283.4 ±160.7 n=5	154.0 n=2	

develop low grade shipping fever can receive veterinary treatment, without risking disqualification on post race sampling.

There is a need for further similar studies, especially those that can follow horses not only to these and similar races and equestrian events, but also on their return home after the additional stress of racing and competition.

ACKNOWLEDGEMENTS

This study was supported by the Chief Executive Major General Watkins of the Royal Hong Kong Jockey Club and his colleagues and staff, through Graham Rock and Andrew Dagnall of Racing World Video Ltd. We wish to express our thanks to them and to all of the veterinary surgeons, owners, trainers and stable staff in Australia, France, Hong Kong, New Zealand, Singapore, the U.K. and the U.S.A. who allowed us access to weigh, examine and blood sample their horses. We also wish to acknowledge the technical support of the laboratory staff of the Equine Veterinary Hospital of the Royal Hong Kong Jockey Club and the Irish Equine Centre.

EFFECTS OF TRANSIT
on the Respiratory System of the Horse

by N. Edward Robinson, BVetMed, MRCVS, PhD

■ Introduction

Recent epidemiological studies identified transportation for more than 500 miles as the most important risk factor for the development of pleuropneumonia in horses (Austin *et al.* 1995; Oikawa and Kusunose 1995). These reports confirmed earlier descriptions of an association between transport and respiratory disease in the horse. Pneumonia has also been induced experimentally by transporting horses for 20 hrs (1858 km). Three of eight horses transported for this period of time showed systemic signs of illness and had pathologic evidence of pneumonia (Oikawa *et al.* 1995).

Respiratory disease is a result either of an increased challenge to the respiratory system by inhaled materials or a reduced ability of the horse to clear these materials. In considering why respiratory disease is associated with transportation, I will review factors that impact on both delivery and clearance. Delivery is dependent on the changes in minute ventilation that are demanded by oxygen delivery and thermoregulation, and on the contaminant load in the air. Defense against challenge by particulates and microorganisms depends on the integrity of the nonspecific clearance mechanisms (the mucociliary system, secretions with antimicrobial properties and phagocytic cells) and specific immune responses. Transport can increase the delivery of foreign materials into the airways and is certainly associated with impaired defenses (Figure 1).

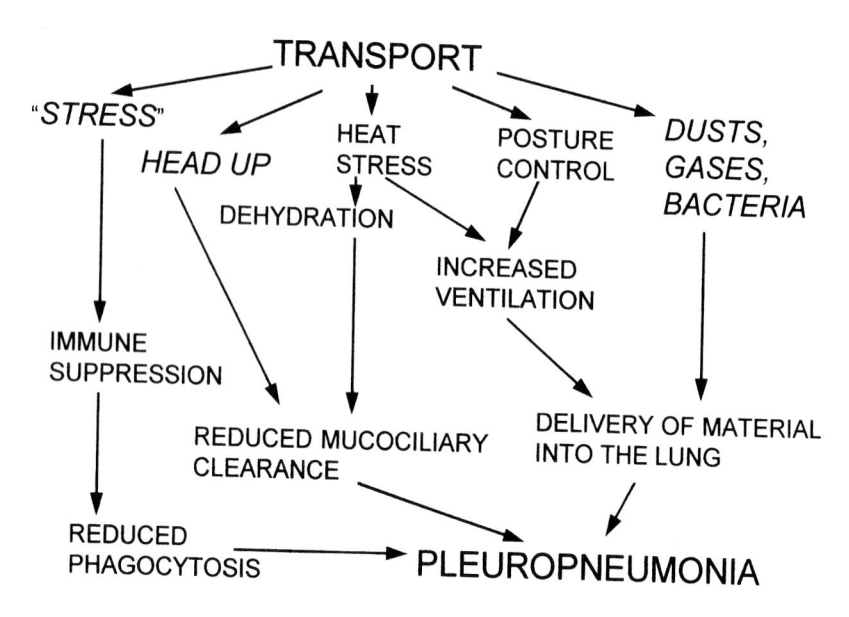

Figure 1. *Factors incriminated in transit-induced respiratory disease in the horse.*

■ Is transportation a form of exercise

Anyone who has tried to stand in a fast-moving vehicle or in a plane during turbulence knows that it takes coordinated activity of postural muscles. This muscular work requires an increase in oxygen consumption, which necessitates an increase in minute ventilation. Perhaps a quadruped is less challenged than a biped by the motion of a travelling vehicle, but horses certainly need to make some postural compensations for acceleration, deceleration and turning of the vehicle. Codazza *et al.* (1974) equated transport with work because the elevations in creatine kinase following transportation were similar to those following a gallop. The design of the transport vehicle would seem to affect the amount of postural compensation; the greater the close confinement, the less need for postural control. However, even when horses are closely confined, they avoid leaning on partitions during transport (Clark *et al.* 1993).

There has been one measurement of the energy expended by equidae during road transport (Doherty *et al.* 1997). Transportation doubled energy consumption over that at rest. Energy consumed during transport was similar to that during a walk.

The preference of horses for facing forward or backward in a trailer has been addressed in several investigations, with the assumption that the horse will prefer the direction that makes postural control easier.

When the horse is allowed to select its travel direction, horses spend more time facing backwards but there is a strong individual preference (Smith *et al.* 1994a; Kusunose and Torikai 1996). However, when confined in a trailer, horses make fewer position shifts and tend to keep their head and neck lower when facing backwards (Clark *et al.* 1993; Smith *et al.* 1994a). If heart rate is taken as an indicator of the work and stress of transportation, there is little difference between facing forward or backward (Clark *et al.* 1993; Smith *et al.* 1994b; Waran *et al.* 1996).

■ Thermoregulation during transport

In the horse, the respiratory system is involved in temperature regulation by participating in both evaporative heat loss and selective cooling of the brain (Hodgson *et al.* 1994; McConaghy *et al.* 1995; Marlin *et al.* 1996). Generally, an increase in ambient temperature is associated with an increase in minute ventilation that is due to an increase in frequency, with tidal volume decreasing concurrently (Kaminski *et al.* 1985). However, the respiratory response to a heat load depends in part on the environmental conditions (Marlin *et al.* 1996). Under hot, dry conditions, horses increase minute ventilation primarily by increasing respiratory frequency. Presumably this causes an increase in deadspace ventilation, which facilitates evaporative heat loss. In warm humid conditions, minute ventilation increases primarily through an increase in tidal volume, which presumably increases alveolar ventilation (Marlin *et al.* 1996).

When horses are transported by road, temperature within the vehicle reflects ambient air conditions if the vehicle is in motion (Smith *et al.* 1996). If the vehicle is left parked, temperature within increases due to the metabolic heat load of the horse and the radiant energy absorbed from the sun. Under the latter conditions, the horse may be exposed to a considerable heat load. Transportation by air or in air-conditioned vehicles probably presents little thermal stress unless the vehicles are parked and the air-conditioning system is turned off (Leadon *et al.* 1990). The increase in temperature in parked aircraft described by Leadon *et al.* would result in approximately a 50 percent increase in minute ventilation.

■ What happens to minute ventilation during transport?

The demand for oxygen by the postural muscles and the need for thermoregulation place ventilatory demands on the respiratory system. I have found no measurements of minute ventilation during transport, but Hobo *et al.* (1995) reported tachypnea without alveolar hyperventilation in transported horses. They attributed these results in part to an effect of the shaking of the truck and in part to an increase in deadspace ventilation necessitated by a need for thermoregulation. However, without a measurement of oxygen consumption or of tidal volume and minute ventilation, it is impossible to determine if horses had an increase in minute ventilation. Any such increase would increase the delivery of airborne contaminants into the lung. If the ambient conditions are hot and humid, or if there is a large muscular demand for oxygen, the accompanying increase in alveolar ventilation will deliver more airborne environmental contaminants deep within the lung.

■ Environmental challenges during transport

Heat is only one of the environmental challenges that can face the horse during transport. Probably more important with regard to the development of disease are the airborne contaminants that can be inhaled into the lung. These include the gases and particulates from the exhaust of the transport vehicle and other vehicles on the road, and the contaminants derived from the environment within the transport vehicle. The latter can include gases, organic dust and its components (particularly microorganisms), and inorganic particulates.

Smith *et al.* (1996) measured the level of ammonia and carbon monoxide in a horse trailer during transport of horses for over 24 hours. Ammonia concentrations (0.81 ± 0.39 ppm; mean ± s.d.) were well below the recommended human exposure limit of 25 ppm (Pickrell 1991). Carbon monoxide levels were highest during the day and lower at night probably reflecting the traffic density around the trailer. Carbon monoxide levels were less than 2 ppm, too low to cause significant interference with oxygen transport. Obviously, the values reported by Smith *et al.* (1996) pertain only to the specific transport conditions of their study. Horse transporters have no control over air pollutants derived from the air outside the vehicle, but they can control the contaminant levels within the vehicle. Ammonia, a respiratory tract irritant and mucus secretagogue (Phipps and Richardson 1976) originates from the breakdown of urea in urine and therefore urine-soaked bedding should be removed regularly.

The respiratory health hazards of agricultural dusts such as those found in association with horses have been the subject of a recent extensive review (Schenker *et al.* 1998). The hazards most likely to be encountered by the transported horse are organic dusts, the composition of which depends on the source material, its origin, and mode of storage. The most important sources of organic dust for horses are the feed and bedding. These can contain plant particles, molds and spores, mycotoxins, bacteria and their components such as endotoxin, mites and insects and their parts, rodent urine, bird droppings, and inorganic dusts derived from the soils on which the plant material was grown.

The horse's exposure to these materials is behavior dependent. When the horse inhales its tidal volume of about 4 liters, it takes air from around its nose, i.e., the breathing zone. Organic dust exposure therefore depends on where the horse has its nose during transport. If the horse is forced to keep its nose close to its hay, dust exposure may be quite high. If however, the horse is free to move away from its feed source, its exposure level may be much less.

When evaluating a horse's exposure to organic dusts, it is essential to sample dusts from the breathing zone, because dust levels can diminish rapidly away from some of the focal sources of organic dust. Woods et al. (1993) demonstrated the importance of this concept by measuring breathing zone and stall dust levels in ponies under two management systems. When ponies ate poor-quality hay and were bedded on straw, breathing zone dust levels averaged 15 to 20 mg/m^3, more than five times higher than the dust levels detected in the stall. When ponies were fed a pelleted diet and bedded on shavings, dust levels were less than 1 mg/m^3 and there was no difference between stall and breathing zone because the focal source of dust had been removed.

The site of deposition of inhaled particles within the respiratory system depends on their size. Particles must be less than 5 microns to be deposited in the lower airways. In the only study to measure airborne particulate levels during horse transport, Smith et al. (1996) reported respirable dust levels of 9 ± 7 mg/m^3, higher than those known to be hazardous to humans and horses. Similar respirable dust levels in the breathing zone are associated with airway inflammation in heaves-susceptible horses (Woods et al. 1993). In humans, levels of 1 to 5 mg/m^3 are the maximum recommended for 8-hour exposure.

Airborne endotoxin levels have not been measured in transport vehicles but have been reported in stables under different management conditions (McGorum et al. 1998). When horses were fed hay, endotoxin levels in respirable dust averaged 1.52 ng/m^3 (range 0.73-25.7). While these levels are considerably lower than those in some piggeries and poultry houses, they are in the range that is reported to cause airway mucosal irritation and bronchospasm (see Schenker et al. [1998] for review).

■ Microbial contamination of the lower airway

Although the bacterial species Pseudomonas, Enterobacter, Flavobacterium, Bacillus, and Corynebacterium, as well as mold genera

Cladosporium, Penicillium, Aspergillus, Alternaria, and Fusarium are found in nearly every air sample collected in barns (Schenker *et al.* 1998), the lower respiratory tract (caudal trachea and beyond) of the healthy horse is normally sterile or contains small numbers of bacteria of low pathogenicity (Blunden and Mackintosh 1991). When the horse is prevented from lowering its head, the bacterial count in the tracheal lavage fluid increases within 24 hours, Pasteurella/Actinobacillus and Streptococcus spp. being the most prevalent (Racklyeft and Love 1990; Raidal *et al.* 1995; Raidal *et al.* 1996). Transportation also is associated with increased numbers of Pasteurella/Actinobacillus and Streptococcus spp. as well as Enterobacteriaceae (Oikawa and Kusunose 1995; Raidal *et al.* 1995; Raidal *et al.* 1996; Oikawa *et al.* 1994). This represents a change in the bacterial population of the airway because Staphylococcus spp. are most common in the healthy horse (Blunden and Mackintosh 1991). Oikawa *et al.* (1995) suggest that Streptococcus spp. originate in the palatine tonsil of the upper airway and may multiply under times of stress and invade the lower airway in which mucociliary clearance is impaired. This is similar to the situation with Pasteurella spp. in cattle and sheep, in which they are the main cause of pleuropneumonia. Other environmental contaminants may also be able to colonize the lung when its defenses are impaired, and it is important to note that in planes transporting horses, the airborne bacterial concentration increases dramatically when the aircraft are parked (Leadon *et al.* 1990).

▪ Clearing inhaled materials

Dusts and microorganisms that are inhaled are cleared by the mucociliary system or removed by phagocytosis. Mucus is a complex mixture of glycoproteins, lipids (surfactant), and water, as well as transudated serum proteins, cells, and associated debris. Mucus secretion is under autonomic control and mucus is released from goblet cells and submucosal glands in response to airway irritation. Mucus secretion is also increased by local release of inflammatory mediators, particularly neutrophil elastase. In this regard, Oikawa *et al.* (1995) noted depletion of mucus from submucosal glands in horses with transport-associated tracheal inflammation. Presumably, increased secretion had exceeded the rate of mucus synthesis. Inflammation also affects mucus secretion by causing mucous cell hyperplasia and makes mucus more viscous and less easy to clear. Gerber *et al.* (1995) demonstrated in the ex vivo horse trachea that the physical properties of mucus are more important than ciliary activity in determining the efficacy of mucociliary clearance.

Mucus hydration is an important determinant of its clearability. During transport, horses drink less and become dehydrated (Smith *et al.* 1996; van den Berg *et al.* 1998). The effect of this dehydration on the physical properties of horse airway mucus has not been determined but it makes good sense to manage horses in a way that minimizes dehydration.

A series of papers by Raidal and coworkers has pointed out the importance of head position in mucociliary transport and the maintenance of respiratory health in horses. When horses were restrained in a stock so that they could not lower their heads for 24 hours, bacterial numbers in a transtracheal aspirate increased from fewer than 10^3 to as high as 10^9 cfu/ml, and the aspirate became more cloudy and contained more neutrophils (over 85 percent at 24 hours). These changes occurred within 6-12 hours in most horses. Allowing horses to lower their heads for 30 mins every 6 hours did not prevent the increase in bacterial numbers. Several horses developed a systemic response that reflected the airway inflammation. After horses were allowed to lower their heads at will, bacterial numbers decreased to control levels over the ensuing 12 hours and evidence of tracheal inflammation waned in parallel (Raidal *et al.* 1995). The increase in bacterial numbers when the head is elevated can be explained in part by posture-associated changes in mucociliary transport rate. Transport rate is most rapid when horses hold their heads down and is reduced by half when the head is elevated. Accumulation of mucoid secretions is associated with a further slowing of transport rate (Raidal *et al.* 1996). A similar gravity-dependent effect on mucus transport velocity has been observed in the horse trachea in vitro (Gerber *et al.* 1996).

Raidal *et al.* (1997) transported horses for 12 hours (983 km) with their heads restrained at a height of approximately 1 meter. After transportation, bacterial numbers in the trachea had increased by five log but were back to normal twelve hours later. The increase in tracheal bacterial count was associated with a systemic response that included an increase in peripheral blood neutrophil count and an increased number of band cells. These changes persisted for up to 36 hours after transport. At the end of transport, five of six horses had abnormal sounds on auscultation of the trachea, and three horses were pyrexic, of which one remained so 36 hours later.

■ The response to inhaled materials

When the airways are challenged by inhaled materials, protective mechanisms are invoked to prevent entry of more materials and eliminate the material. Immediate responses that are neurally mediated

EFFECTS OF TRANSIT
on the Immune System of the Horse

by Melissa T. Hines, DVM, PhD, Diplomate ACVIM

■ Summary

Stress induced immunosuppression is thought to be one of the factors responsible for the increased incidence of infectious disease associated with transport. While several studies have documented that transport can be stressful for horses, it is often difficult to quantitate stress and its effects. Although a relationship between stress and immunity clearly exists, the inherent complexity of the immune system and variability in experimental design make it difficult to draw firm conclusions concerning the effects of transport on immunity in horses. This paper reviews the literature examining the association between transport and immunity.

■ Effects on pulmonary immunity

Respiratory tract disease is probably the most common form of disease following the transport of horses. Transport may routinely increase bacterial challenge in the lower respiratory tract and has been identified as a risk factor for pleuropneumonia (Anderson *et al.* 1985; Austin *et al.* 1995; Raidal *et al.* 1997). Since the pulmonary immune response is at least partially distinct from the systemic response, many research efforts have specifically focused on defining the effects of transport on pulmonary immunity. Unfortunately, current knowledge regarding the mechanisms of pulmonary immunity in horses remains limited. Typically, most studies have utilized evaluation of respiratory secretions obtained by either bronchoalveolar lavage (BAL) or transtracheal aspiration (Figure 1). While these methods often yield large variations in cell populations and may not completely reflect the response within the pulmonary parenchyma, they remain the most practical means of assessing pulmonary immunity in horses.

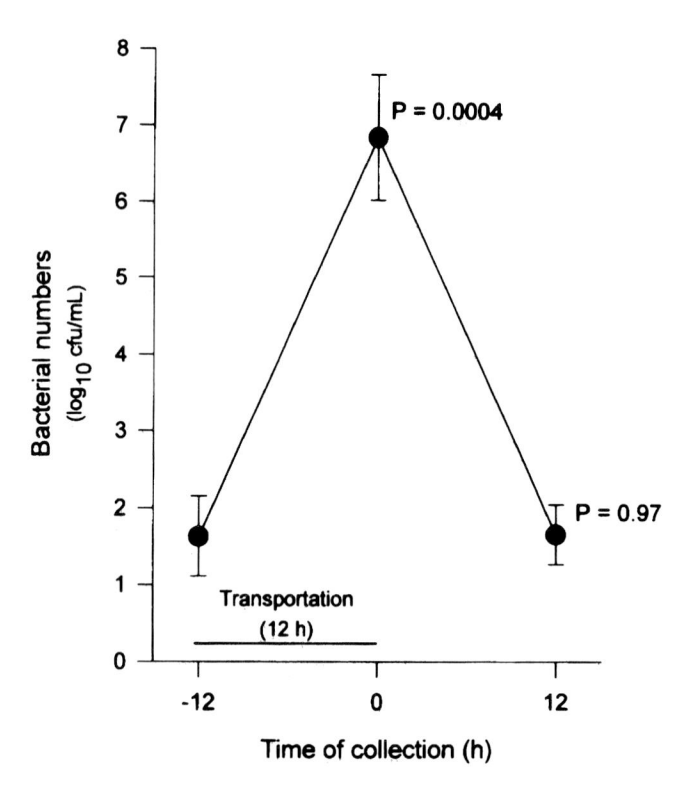

Figure 3: *Bacterial numbers (mean +/- standard error, following $\log^{10}$ transformation) in transtracheal aspirates from horses prior to (-12 h), immediately (0 h) and 12 h after transportation. [Reprinted with permission from Raidal, S.L., Bailey, G.D., Love, D.N. (1997) Effect of transportation on lower respiratory tract contamination and peripheral blood neutrophil function. Aust. Vet. J. 75, 433-438.]*

However, bacterial numbers significantly increased after transportation (Figure 3). In addition, relative to earlier studies of confinement with head elevation alone, the mean number of bacteria was greater, suggesting either an increased number of bacteria aspirated or impaired pulmonary clearance mechanisms. The bacteria were cleared rapidly after transport, with numbers returning to pre-transport levels by 12 hours. The type of bacteria isolated after transport also varied from those isolated after head elevation alone, with increased numbers of bacteria from the *Enterbacteriaceae* family being isolated following transport. This may reflect stress-induced changes in pharyngeal microflora or the types of bacteria in the transport environment.

The functional activity of alveolar macrophages following transport has also been assessed. An important first line of defense in the distal airways and alveolar spaces, macrophages function not only in the phagocytosis of particles and microorganisms, but also in the secretion of cytokines

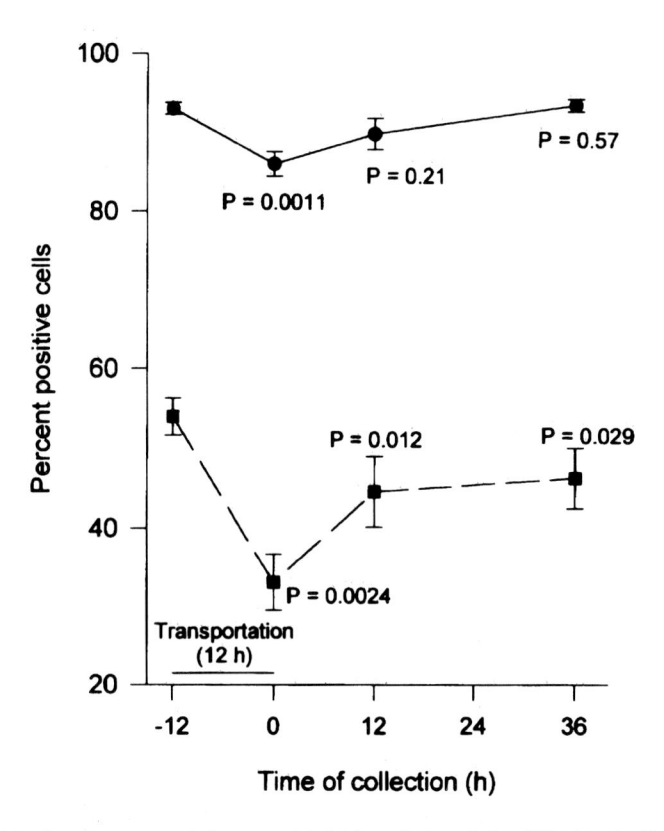

Figure 4: *Phagocytosis of fluorescent-labeled bacteria by peripheral blood neutrophils prior to (-12 h) and immediately (0 h), 12 h and 36 h after transportation. Values given are the mean (+/- standard error) percentage of cells positive for attachment (●) and internalization (■). [Reprinted with permission from Raidal, S.L., Bailey, G.D., Love, D.N. (1997) Effect of transportation on lower respiratory tract contamination and peripheral blood neutrophil function. Aust. Vet. J. 75, 433-438.]*

and in regulation of the immune response. In the study by Traub-Dargatz et al. (1988), transport did not affect the phagocytosis of *Streptococcus faecalis* by pulmonary alveolar macrophages. Crisman et al. (1992) also concluded that there was no significant change in either the phagocytic or the bactericidal capacity of pulmonary alveolar macrophages due to transport, although some differences were observed. Similarly, in a study by Oikawa and coworkers (1999) in which horses were shipped for 38 hours by road, there were no changes in pulmonary alveolar macrophage functions either in horses with or those without pyrexia. Thus, studies to date have failed to document impaired function of pulmonary alveolar macrophages following transport.

■ Effects on systemic immunity

Studies on the effects of transport on specific aspects of systemic immunity in horses have been limited. Although changes in leukocyte counts port (Mudron *et al.* 1994). In a study of transportation and weaning, calves were immunized with keyhole limpet haemocyanin and serum concentrations of antigen-specific IgG1, IgG2, IgA and IgM measured (Mackenzie *et al.* 1997). Results were variable depending on antibody class and time post-stress.

▪ Possible mechanisms of transport-related immunosuppression

The mechanisms responsible for the effects of stress on the immune system are complex. Neuroendocrine hormones, particularly glucocorticoids, are believed to play a primary role. Generally, transport has been shown to cause an increase in the circulating concentration of cortisol in several species, including horses (Dalin *et al.* 1993; Murata *et al.* 1987; Smith *et al.* 1996). While corticosteroids undoubtedly alter host defenses and increase the incidence of infectious diseases, the extent of the immunosuppression and the specific mechanisms involved vary depending on a number of factors, such as species, age, and state of activation of the immune system. Specific information related to the horse remains limited, but probable mechanisms of immunosuppression include changes in leukocyte kinetics, inhibition of macrophage function, decreased MHC class II expression, decreased secretion of interleukin-2 and gamma interferon, and decreased $CD4^+$ T cell activation.

Catecholamines can also increase in response to transit stress and have been linked to alterations in the immune system (Dalin *et al.* 1993). They are known to influence leukocyte kinetics, inhibit B and T cell proliferative responses to mitogens, and diminish natural killer cell function.

A variety of other substances, including numerous cytokines, arachidonic acid metabolites, and prolactin, may be involved in the modification of immune function by stress. Interestingly, prostaglandin E2 may suppress macrophage function and inhibit natural killer cell activity. Although transport was not involved, ozone exposure increased susceptibility of mice to respiratory infection with *Streptococcus zooepidemicus* (Gilmour *et al.* 1993). Pretreatment with the non-steroidal anti-inflammatory drug indomethacin blunted the increase of prostaglandin E2 in BALF luid and reduced mortality.

Surfactant also influences pulmonary defense mechanisms. As glucocorticoids and catecholamines may increase surfactant production, Crisman *et al.* (1992) speculated that the concentration of lipid in BALF might correlate with the level of stress. However, BALF lipid concentrations did not change in response to either transport or repeated lavage. Hobo, Oikawa and coworkers measured concentrations of specific surfactant components in BALF, and found that the concentrations of phosphatidylglycerol and surfactant proteins A and D decreased following transport, indicating a reduction in the quantity of surfactant (Hobo *et al.* 1997; Oikawa and Jones 1999). A decline in surfactant, due to either a decreased production by the alveolar type II epithelial cells or an increased utilization/removal, could impair defense mechanisms in the lung.

■ Intervention/future directions

Transit of horses is clearly associated with an increased susceptibility to disease. However, the role that immunosuppression plays relative to other factors in this increased susceptibility remains unclear. Studies to date have shown a number of changes, but results have been inconsistent. Factors such as the length of transport, type of transport and previous experience of the horse all influence the degree of stress. In addition, the complexity of the immune system and limitations in our ability to adequately assess many components add to the difficulty in determining the significance of changes to overall immunocompetence and the development of disease. One important question for future studies is what is the relevant immune response? Also, should studies be antigen specific and if so, which antigens are of importance?

The ultimate goal of understanding the mechanisms of transport induced immunosuppression is to develop strategies for decreasing the incidence of disease in transported horses. Relatively basic approaches, such as minimizing stress and careful monitoring of animals, are critical. The benefits of prophylactic use of drugs such as antibiotics or non-steroidal anti-inflammatory drugs are unclear. In studies of confinement with head elevation by Raidal *et al.* (1997), the administration of penicillin did not reliably reduce bacterial numbers or prevent the accumulation of purulent lower respiratory tract secretions, although numbers of beta-haemolytic *Streptococcus* spp. were reduced.

Other potential means of intervention include the use of nutritional management (Vitamin E), cytokines or non-specific immunomodulators. Vitamin E administration did not affect serum immunoglobulin concentrations, leucocyte function or cortisol concentrations in transported calves (Mudron *et al.* 1994). However, supplementation with vitamin E or vitamin E and selenium has been shown to enhance the humoral immune response to novel antigens in horses, and may have more widespread positive effects on immunity (Baalsrud and Overnes 1986). Interferon-alpha, a cytokine with antiviral, immunomodulatory and antiproliferative activity, has many potential applications, including reducing pulmonary inflammation in horses with chronic inflammatory airway disease and aiding in control of the bovine respiratory disease complex in calves (Moore 1996). While there are currently no data to support the efficacy of interferon-alpha in the prevention or treatment of transport associated respiratory tract disease in horses, anecdotal reports suggest that it may be beneficial, and this area warrants further investigation. Alterations in both the pulmonary and systemic immune systems have been demonstrated following the administration of an immunostimulant (inactivated *Propionibacterium acnes*) to young horses, but it is unknown whether such agents would be of significant benefit in reducing transport associated respiratory disease (Flaminio *et al.* 1998). Further research is needed in order to better define the effects of transport stress on immunity and to evaluate potential means of intervention.

DOES TRANSPORT STRESS AFFECT EXERCISE PERFORMANCE in Horses?

By L. Jill McCutcheon, DVM, PhD &
Raymond J. Geor, BVSc, MVSc, Diplomate ACVIM

■ Introduction

An increasing number of horses are transported over long distances in order to compete in national and international events. The expectations placed on equine athletes at competitions of this caliber has led to heightened interest in the effects of such transport on exercise performance in the subsequent competitions. Rapid, long distance transportation of horses, whether by road, rail, or air results in alterations in environmental conditions and in patterns of food and water intake, exercise, and sleep. Furthermore, when travel to competitions requires horses to be transported across several time zones, there is also the potential for physiological alterations arising from the disruption of circadian rhythms as a result of the transmeridian translocation (jet lag). While there are several studies in horses that have examined one or more of the potentially detrimental aspects of transport, there is a paucity of information that directly addresses the question of what effects these stresses may impose on subsequent exercise performance. Accordingly, supporting information from the more extensive literature describing investigations involving human workers and athletes, forms part of the background of this discussion.

■ What constitutes transport stress for the horse?

There are two main components to the stress imposed on horses that are transported. The first is the duration of the transit period. Regardless of the stressors inherent to the type(s) of transportation utilized, it is the length of time over which horses are subjected to transit stresses that will contribute most significantly to their effect. The other major component of transport stress for the horse is the potential for desynchronisation of body rhythms as a result of crossing time zones during air travel (jet lag). In these circumstances, the horse is subject to the disruption of biological rhythms such as those associated with body temperature, heart rate, cortisol production, sleep and activity patterns (Evans *et al.* 1978; Houpt 1980; Irvine and Alexander 1994; Kaseda and Ogawa 1992; Luna 1993).

The stressors associated with transportation of horses arise from changes in environment, feeding, exercise, and sleep patterns prior to, during and following their translocation. The interactive effects of the noise, vibration, confinement, constant motion, possible dehydration and caloric deficits, and anxiety, as well as the disruption of normal circadian rhythms attendant to transmeridian air travel can contribute to the detrimental effects of transit. Often, the route will entail travel by road prior to and following air transportation. The type and dimensions of vehicle utilized, road surface, distance traveled, environmental conditions, number of stops, availability of feed and water, and disposition and experience of the horse in terms of both loading and transport should be considered when assessing the effects of transport by road.

Travel by air may be in a predominantly north-south direction (translatitudinal) but often involves movement eastward or westward across several time zones. In such instances, superimposed upon an unfamiliar setting, possible variations in environmental temperature and humidity, and prolonged restriction of movement imposed by crates will be a shift in the internal biological clock. This phase shift results in a transient desynchronisation of biological rhythms lasting until the biological rhythms adjust to the new environmental conditions (Klein *et al.* 1972). Depending on the direction of travel, individual circadian rhythms are advanced or delayed in both duration and phase and require time for re-entrainment, with different rhythms possibly re-entraining at different rates. In humans, the subjective symptoms of jet lag usually include fatigue, sleep disorders, difficulties in concentrating, irritability, depression, disorientation, distorted estimation of time, space and distance, lightheadedness, loss of appetite, and gastrointestinal disorders, all of which have been documented in air crew personnel studies (Manfredini *et al.* 1998; Wright *et al.* 1983).

Given the numerous negative aspects of jet lag, it would be logical to suggest that work or exercise performance is detrimentally affected by transmeridian travel. To address this question, numerous investigators have examined the effects of air travel on one or more specific measures of performance capacity in humans.

■ What is known about effects of travel on performance capacity in human athletes/workers?

There are conflicting reports as to the effects of travel and/or disruptions of biological rhythms on human physical performance capacity. These reports include investigations of individual and team athletes, shift workers, and jet aircraft and manned space vehicle crews. While there are numerous subjective, empirical accounts of decrements in exercise performance, qualitative or quantitative documentation of these effects is relatively limited (Wright *et al.* 1983). In part, this lack of objective data can be explained by difficulties in the design and conduct of controlled experimental studies.

In sports events, difficulty in controlling for environmental and scheduling factors may result in performance variability, irrespective of the influence of travel. For example, there is evidence that in events such as sprinting, cycling and discus throwing, performance is better in the evening than in the morning, a time that coincides with the peaking of certain biological rhythms such as body temperature. However, this interpretation may be confounded by the fact that, for sprint events, the higher environmental temperatures in late afternoon/early evening may be favorable for record-breaking performances. For weight throwers, wind speed and direction may also be more conducive to a winning performance at this time of day (Atkinson and Reilly 1996). In addition, although transmeridian travel to an event could affect performance, it becomes difficult to investigate the negative effects of desynchronisation of circadian rhythms in competitive athletes because of the masking of negative effects of stress, fatigue caused by the flight itself, and the forced situation of competing in a unfamiliar environment.

Some of this variance in measurement of performance is removed in more controlled environments employed in studies of military recruits and airline and spacecraft crew. Following eastward or westward travel across 6-9 time zones, or after north-south flights of equivalent length, significant deterioration in the performance of these personnel was

■ 270 m sprint
▨ 2.8 km run

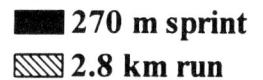

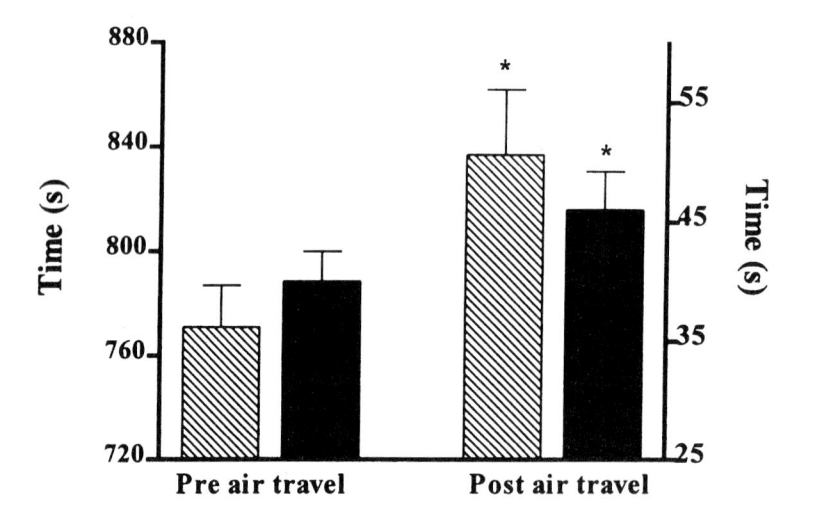

(adapted from Wright et al. 1983)

Figure 1. *Performance of military recruits (n = 15) in exercise tests consisting of a 270 m sprint and a 2.8 km endurance run before and after trans Atlantic air travel.*
* = *significantly different from pre air travel exercise test (P< 0.05).*

only noted after travel in an eastward direction (Hauty and Adams 1966; Wright *et al.* 1983). Eastward flights are associated with a phase advance and the mean re-entrainment rate for the shift in biological rhythms is approximately 50% slower than following westward travel. Full readjustment after 6-9 h of eastward flight can require as much as 8 days compared to 3 days for readjustment following a westward flight. On the other hand, westward flights, characterised by a phase delay, are followed by a more rapid recovery and resynchronisation of the biological clock and have less effect on sleep quality. In the military personnel, there were performance decrements of 3-4% in both simple tasks such as reaction time and in more complex sensorimotor skills after eastward flights (Klein and Wegmann 1974). When recruits were tested for 5 days before and after eastward deployment across 6 time zones, cardiorespiratory function during submaximal and maximal exercise, and isometric strength of the upper torso, legs and trunk extensor muscles was unaffected. In contrast, there was post-flight performance deterioration in dynamic arm strength (6.1-10.8%), elbow flexor strength (13.3%), lifting (9.5%), and sprint (270 m) (8.4-25%) and endurance (2.8 km) run times (9%) when compared to preflight tests (Wright *et al.* 1983). (Figure 1.) The number of days during which performance is affected may vary. In a recent study, Reilly and colleagues (Reilly *et al.* 1997) reported that in British Olympic squad members, several performance measures (leg and back strength, reaction time, subjective jet lag symptoms) were impaired for five days after 7 h of transmeridian air travel.

■ Mechanisms underlying decrements in human performance following transmeridian travel

The most universally accepted mechanism to explain performance decrements following travel is the disruption in circadian rhythms that underlie the symptoms of jet lag. The circadian rhythms that could contribute to altered performance are numerous and are affected to different degrees by a phase shift in the sleep-wake cycle. Such biological rhythms include body temperature, the cardiovascular system (blood pressure, heart rate), ventilation, gastrointestinal function, mood states, hormonal secretions (adrenaline, noradrenaline, growth hormone, and cortisol), and metabolic variables such as oxygen consumption at rest and glucose metabolism (Atkinson and Reilly 1996). Attempts to predict the extent of potentially detrimental effects of jet lag caused by circadian rhythm disruption are confounded by several factors. First, there is considerable variability in the rate of readaptation between individuals; 25-30% of transmeridian travelers have little difficulty in readjustment while an equal percentage adjust poorly (Winget *et al.* 1984). Secondly, there is also a seasonal effect associated with recovery from jet lag. Re-entrainment after transmeridian flights is more rapid in summer than in winter, possibly because the longer day permits greater exposure to natural daylight (Suvanto and Harma 1993). In addition, rhythmic readaptation has been demonstrated to vary according to rhythm amplitude, behavioral traits, age, motivation, and sleep habits (Atkinson *et al.* 1993; Mejean *et al.* 1992; Monk 1992). This variability in patterns of readjustment has contributed to the widely varying results of studies examining the effects of transmeridian travel on sports performance.

There is considerable evidence that timing of an event in relation to various circadian rhythms may influence its outcome. In human subjects, taking advantage of circadian rhythms has been demonstrated to produce major benefits in tasks involving endurance, mental function, and physical strength. Selecting the best time of day (with respect to circadian rhythms) can result in as much as a 10% increase in athletic performance (Manfredini *et al.* 1998). For instance, the peaking of body temperature in late afternoon (~0.5 to 0.8°C higher than the 24 h nadir) contributes to improvements in performance by decreasing study of military personnel reported a reduction in sleep disturbances with the use of such diets (Graeber 1982), a clear link between diet and jet lag has not been established.

The phase shift in the sleep-wake cycle noted after transmeridian flight has led to studies of phototherapy as a means to reduce the effects of jet lag. Exposure to bright light, with specified intensity, duration, and timing to advance or delay the phase of some circadian rhythms has been attempted. Phototherapy has been reported to result in consolidation of sleep into a single episode after phototherapy (Cole and Kripke 1989), and to accelerate circadian re-entrainment (Sasaki *et al.* 1989). However, there is still insufficient data on the effectiveness of this therapy. The Consensus Report for Light Treatment for Sleep Disorders concludes that "much remains to be learned before procedures can be developed that are at once effective, reliable, and practical. For this to happen, optimal combinations of several light exposure parameters must first be defined and tailored to specific flight situations" (Boulos *et al.* 1995).

Administered at the appropriate time of day, several drugs can specifically alter some aspect of biological time structure (chronobiotic drugs). However, inconsistent or inconclusive results have been produced by several such chronobiotic drugs including barbituates, alcohol, serotinin-depleting tranquilisers, and corticosteroids. In recent years, melatonin (N-acetyl-5-methoxytryptamine), a chronomodulating hormone normally secreted at night by the pineal gland, has received much attention. In most animals, melatonin serves to transmit information about the light/dark cycle to the body. Whereas the biological clock normally facilitates daytime activity by raising body temperature and plasma adrenaline, the rise in plasma melatonin in early evening contributes to drowsiness and feelings of fatigue (Dawson and Encel 1993; Lavie *et al.* 1997). Thus, the timing of melatonin ingestion affects the degree and direction of its effect, with ingestion in the morning producing a delay and in the late afternoon/early evening an advance, of the body clock (Krauchi *et al.* 1997; Lewy *et al.* 1980). Evening ingestion of melatonin in the new time zone has proven effective against jet lag in several studies. Arendt *et al.* 1987 reported a reduction in the negative feelings of jet lag and increased subjective alertness, reduced sleep onset latency and improved sleep quality after administration of melatonin for 14 days after westward flight. However, because of its potentially sedative effects, there are contradictory reports as to residual effects of melatonin on alertness and mental performance (Arendt *et al.* 1987; Atkinson *et al.* 1997; Waterhouse *et al.* 1998). Consequently, although there is evidence for the efficacy of melatonin in reducing symptoms of fatigue following air travel, it is less clear that its beneficial effects extend to promoting performance.

■ What is known about effects of long distance transport exercise performance in equine athletes?

There is little doubt that prolonged exposure to a combination of stresses during long distance travel can have negative consequences for horses. However, surprisingly little is known about the effects of such long distance transport on subsequent exercise performance in equine athletes. Anecdotally, some trainers have timed the transport of racehorses from Europe to North America such that there is as little as 1-2 days between travel and the race time, citing subsequent decrements in performance for days to weeks following travel as their rationale (O'Connor *et al.* 1991). In the preceding discussion, many of the factors that could contribute to decrements in performance capacity have been described. However, there are very few studies that have examined whether any of these factors result in altered performance in the horse. In a study of the effects of transport on muscle function, 40 young (3-5 years old) thoroughbred horses were transported 300 km by road (Codazza *et al.* 1974). The investigators reported that the effects of the transport on some serum enzymes activities 2 days following transport were similar to those induced by a 1,500 m canter. Similarly, 10 thoroughbred horses which had recently run races were subjected to time trials one week prior to and two hours after being transported 129 km in 2.5 hours (Japanese Equine Research Institute 1977). In the trials, running time for 1400m, and post exercise heart rate and respiratory rate were not different. In several of the studies that have been undertaken, the intensity of exercise or the length of the transit period is insufficient to shed light on performance decrements that may arise following long distance transport (Beaunoyer and Chapman 1987). The following discussion suggests factors most likely to manifest as performance decrements, supported by the evidence that has been provided by studies in the horse.

■ Fluid losses

As previously mentioned, transport will result in changes in environment, food and water intake, and sleep and activity patterns (Smith *et al.* 1996). Losses of body weight are the commonest physiological effect of transport and reports from several studies approximate the decrease in body weight (BW) during long distance transit at approximately 0.45 to 0.55% BW/h regardless of the whether it is transport by road or air (Mars *et al.* 1992; van den Berg *et al.* 1998; D. J. Marlin, per-

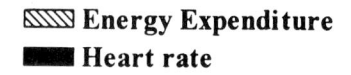

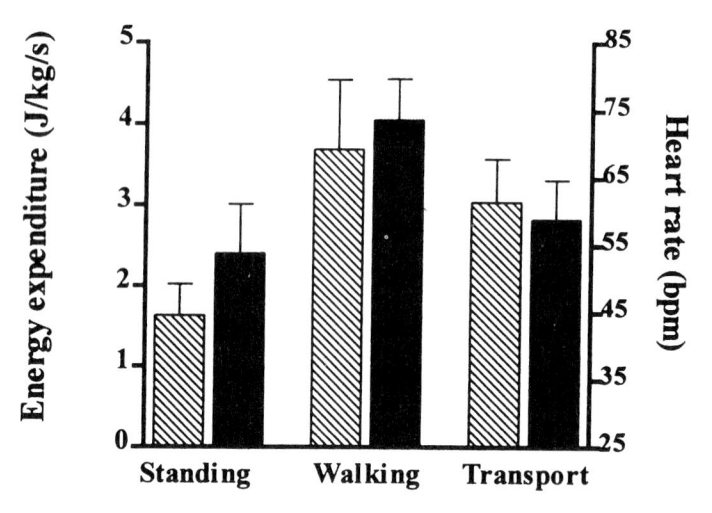

(adapted from Doherty et al. 1997)

Figure 2. *Comparison of heart rate and energy expenditure in Shetland Ponies (n = 5) at rest, while walking and during 30 min of transport.*

sonal communication). Friend and coworkers (Friend *et al.* 1998) reported a 30-40 kg change in body mass in horses transported 24 hr by road in hot conditions (29-35°C, 30-95% RH). Although horses were unloaded and offered water every 4 h, there was a 50% reduction in water consumption compared to controls. Importantly, much of the fluid losses associated with transport can be regained very quickly post transport when horses have access to palatable water. In a study by van den Berg *et al* (van den Berg *et al.* 1998), horses that were 3% dehydrated (as determined by change in body mass) following 600 km of road travel in hot conditions corrected this deficit within 1 h following transport. Thus, efforts to minimize the potential for hot, dusty, or changeable environmental conditions will decrease the extent of fluid losses due to evaporative cooling as well as reducing the risk of respiratory disease. Providing access to water during and following transport should reduce the extent and minimize the effects of fluid losses.

The significance of changes in body mass due to reduced water and feed intake and/or evaporative losses on subsequent performance will depend on several factors. The willingness of the horse to eat and drink following transport will affect the rate of rehydration and the rate of increase in body mass. The re-establishment of gut fill lost during transport will also increase the associated fluid reservoir. Thus, the time available before training or competition is to be resumed and the nature of the event should be considered. While it may be argued that a 1-3% body mass loss poses little or no disadvantage for a short term high intensity event, the same would not be true for more prolonged exercise. The interactive effects of dehydration, prolonged exercise and high environmental temperature can seriously affect performance capacity. One important feature that might be considered part of transport stress is the post-travel adjustment to a new environment. Potentially, the extent to which an unfamiliar environment may affect the rate of readjustment after transport is not effectively reproduced under laboratory conditions or in circumstances under which horses return to their original point of departure.

■ Energy expenditures and caloric deficits

Although decreases in body mass resulting from transport may largely reflect fluid losses, reductions in feed intake during and following transport also contribute to these losses. Compounding the reduction in feed intake is the energy expenditure required during transit. Although movement is restricted, there is evidence that horses expend a significant quantity of energy during transit. The work of Doherty and colleagues (Doherty *et al.* 1997) demonstrated that the average heart rate and energy expenditure in Shetland ponies during trailering was equivalent to that required by walking (Figure 2). Obviously, horses that are anxious or excitable travelers are likely to consume less food and water and expend considerably more energy during transit than a calmer horse. Similarly, rough or winding roads or turbulent air travel that demands continuous adjustments by the horse in order to maintain balance will increase energy demands and the degree of muscular fatigue. A number of studies have examined whether the orientation of the horse in the trailer (forward or backward facing) alters the horse's response to transport in terms of the effects of acceleration and deceleration on its center of mass and stability as well as the stress of transport as determined by heart rate. In one study, lower values for heart rate and energy expenditure, based on the orientation of horses within the van or trailer, were determined when horses were rearward facing during transit (Waran 1997). In contrast however, Smith and coworkers were not able to determine differences in heart rate when comparing the transport of horses in trailers while facing forward or backward (Smith *et al.* 1994). Studies in sleep-deprived human subjects have demonstrated depletion in muscle glycogen, particularly within type I fibers of postural muscles. It is likely that prolonged periods of transport requiring frequent postural adjustments will also lead to significant decrements in muscle glycogen content. When combined with a reduction in glycogen resynthesis resulting from decreased energy intake, it is possible that the energy expenditure and caloric deficits incurred during transport could adversely affect exercise performance.

■ Disruptions to circadian rhythm

Perhaps the least is known about the potential effects of jet lag on subsequent equine performance. It is known that a 6 to 9 h flight can cause a reversal of the normal daily variation in rectal temperature and alterations in the day vs. night water intake pattern for 48 to 72 h following transport (D. Martin, personal communication). The extent to which other circadian rhythms such as catecholamine and cortisol secretion, gastrointestinal function, and sleep patterns are altered is not well understood. Further work is required to determine how disruptions in circadian rhythms caused by advances or delays in the sleep-wake cycle can directly or indirectly affect performance.

■ Research directions

The paucity of data on the effects of transport on equine performance hinders our ability to make specific recommendations. The efficacy of any recommendations should be based on scientifically defensible research. In considering the effects of transport on performance, there are several questions that need to be asked:

(1) What are appropriate measures of performance that can be evaluated pre- and post-transport? Many of the measures of performance used in human subjects cannot be adequately measured in equine athletes (e.g. hand, arm, leg, and back strength, reaction time, accuracy, time to complete pre-determined exercise protocol). In addition, wide test-retest variability for sprint and endurance exercise performance (i.e. run time to fatigue) limits the usefulness of these measures in the assessment of "performance". A more rational approach would be to use exercise protocols as a means to test hypotheses concerning the effects of "transport stress" on physiological responses to exercise.

(2) What are the effects of transportation vs. the effects of the disruptions to circadian rhythm on performance? From the preceding discussion, it is clear that different stressors fall under the umbrella of "transport stress". Therefore, some thought must be given as to the aspect of transport stress that most warrants investigation. Prolonged road transport vs. air travel likely imposes different physiological stressors and the impact of these transport modes on subsequent exercise responses also may differ. Ideally, studies should investigate the effects of both of these forms of transport stress.

The first step in such studies would be to determine whether and to what extent transmeridian travel causes desynchronisation of circadian rhythms in the horse. If significant desynchronisation is evident, then further studies to determine the effects of "jet lag" on exercise performance would be warranted.

It has been possible to simulate a phase-shift by altering the light/dark stimulus in studies of human subjects. Therefore it may be possible to simulate an abrupt phase shift for the horse. While such a simulation may be possible, it might prove no less expensive than actually transporting horses. In addition, there may be difficulties in predicting expected results under simulated conditions compared to those following transmeridian flight. Apparently, the asymmetry noted in the time necessary for re-entrainment after eastward vs. westward flight has been observed to be reversed when human subjects are studied under controlled laboratory vs. postflight conditions. In order to have the best opportunity to determine physiological alterations consistent with disruption of circadian rhythms, a flight that imposes a 9 to 12 h advance or delay for the biological time clock is warranted.

Baucus, K.L., Squires, E.L., Ralston, S.L., McKinnon, A.O. and Nett, T.M. (1990a) *Effect of transportation on the estrous cycle and concentrations of hormones in mares.* J. Anim. Sci. 68: 419-426.

Baucus, K.L., Ralston, S.L., Nockels, C.F., McKinnon, A.O. and Squires, E.L. (1990b) *Effects of transportation on early embryonic death in mares.* J. Anim. Sci. 68: 345-351.

Bayly, W.M., Liggit, H.D., Houston, W. and Laegreid, W.W. (1986) *Stress and effect on equine pulmonary mucosal defenses.* In: Proc. 32nd Ann. Conf. AAEP, 32: 253-262.

Clark, D.K., Friend, T.H. and Dellmeier, G. (1993) *The effect of orientation during trailer transport on heart rate, cortisol and balance in horses.* Appl. Anim. Behav. Sci. 38: 179-189.

Codazza, D., Genchi, C., Agnes, F. and Maffeo, G. (1974) *Serum enzyme changes and haemato-chemical levels in Thoroughbreds after transport and exercise.* J. So. Afr. Vet. Assn. 45: 331-334.

Cregier, S. (1982) *Reducing equine hauling stress: a review.* J. Equine Vet. Sci. 2: 186-198.

Crisman, M.V., Hodgson, D.R., Bayly, W.M. and Liggitt, H.D. (1992) *Effects of transport on constituents of bronchoalveolar lavage fluid from horses.* Cornell Vet. 82: 233-246.

Doherty, O., Booth, M., Waran, N., Salthouse, C. and Cuddeford, D. (1997) *Study of the heart rate and energy expenditure of ponies during transport.* Vet. Rec. 23: 589-592.

* Equine Research Institute, Japan Racing Association. (1997) *Effect of road transportation between Miho Training Center and Tokyo Race Track on athletic performance in racehorses.* Juui Gijutsu 15: 501-565 (written in Japanese).

Ferlazzo, A., Panzera, S.M. and Caola, G. (1983) *Serum hemato-chemical parameters in Equus asinus L. - influence of transport stress.* Clin. Vet. 106: 238-242.

Ferlazzo, A., Caola, G., Omero, A. and Panzera, M. (1984) *Serum enzymes in the unexercised horse after transport.* Arch. Vet. Ital. 35: 27-31.

Foss, M.A. (1996) *Effects of trailer transport duration on body weight and blood biochemical variables of horses.* Pferdeheilkunde 12: 435-437.

Friend, T.H., Martin, M.T., Householder, D.D. and Bushong, D.M. (1998) *Stress responses of horses during a long period of transport in a commercial truck.* JAVMA 212: 838-844.

Grandin, T. (1993) *Livestock Handling and Transport.* CAB International, Wallingford, UK, 320 pp.

Hayakawa, Y., Komae, H., Ide, H., Nakagawa, H., Yoshida, Y., Kamada, M., Kataoka, Y. and Nakazawa, M. (1993) *An occurrence of equine transport pneumonia caused by mixed infection with Pasteurella caballi, Streptococcus suis and Streptococcus zooepidemicus.* J. Vet. Med. Sci. 55: 455-456.

* Hirano, S. (1994) *Incidence of shipping fever in racehorses transported by road for 1000-1300 km.* Equine Sci. 31: 445 (written in Japanese).

* Hobo, S., Kuwano, A. and Oikawa, M. (1995) *Respiratory changes in horses during automobile transportation.* J. Equine Sci. 6: 135-139.

* Hobo, S., Oikawa, M., Kuwano, A., Yoshida, K. and Yoshihara, T. (1997) *Effect of transportation on the composition of bronchoalveolar lavage fluid obtained from horses.* Am. J. Vet. Res. 58: 531-534.

* Hobo, S., Ogasawara, Y., Kuroki, Y., Akino, T. and Yoshihara, T. (1999a) *Purification and biochemical characterization of pulmonary surfactant protein A of horses.* Am. J. Vet. Res. 60:169-173.

* Hobo, S., Ogasawara, Y., Kuroki, Y., Akino, T. and Yoshihara, T. (1999b) *Purification and biochemical characterization of equine pulmonary surfactant protein D.* Am. J. Vet. Res. 60:368-372.

* Hobo, S. Kondo, T. and Yoshihara, T. (1999c) *Development and application of two-site sandwich enzyme-linked immunosorbent assay for equine pulmonary surfactant protein A.* Am. J. Vet. Res. (in press).

* Hobo, S. and Yoshihara, T. (1999d) *Development and application of enzyme-linked immunosorbent assay for equine pulmonary surfactant protein D.* Am. J. Vet. Res. (submitted).

* Hobo, S. and Yoshihara, T. (1999e) *Development and application of enzyme-linked immunosorbent assay for equine pulmonary surfactant protein A in sera.* Am. J. Vet. Res. (submitted).

Houpt, K.A. (1986) *Stable vices and trailer problems.* Vet. Clin. N. Amer. Equine Pract. 2: 623- 633.

Houpt, K.A. Lieb, S. and Grandin, T. (1993) *Horse handling and ransport.* In: Grandin, T. ed., Livestock Handling and Transport, CAB International, Wallingford, UK, pp. 233-252.

* Ishida, N. Hobo, S., Takahashi, T., Nambo, Y., Sato, F., Hasegawa, T. and Mukoyama, H. (1999) *Chronological changes in superoxide-scavenging ability and lipid peroxide concentration of equine serum due to stress from exercise and transport.* Equine vet. J., Suppl. 29. (in press).

* Ito, S., Fujii, Y., Uchiyama, T. and Kaneko, M. (1992) *Four cases of rhabdomyolysis in the Thoroughbred during transportation.* Bull. Equine Res. Inst. 29: 1-5 (written in Japanese with English summary, tables and figures).

* Japan Racing Association. (1997) *Annual report on racehorse hygiene* (written both in Japanese and English).

* Kamada, M. and Akiyama, Y. (1974) *Studies on the distribution of Streptococcus zooepidemicus in equine respiratory tracts.* Exp. Rep. Equine Health Lab. 11: 152-154.

* Katayama, Y., Oikawa, M., Yoshihara, T., Kuwano, A. and Hobo, S. (1995) *Clinico-Pathological effects of atmospheric ammonia exposure on horses.* J. Equine Sci. 6: 99-104.

* Kawamoto, K., Sato, H., Oikawa, M., Yoshihara, T., Kaneko, M. and Matsuda, H. (1996) *Nerve growth factor activity detected in equine peripheral blood of horses with fever after truck transportation.* J. Equine Sci. 7: 43-46.

* Kusunose, R. and Torikai, K. (1996) *Behavior of untethered horses during vehicle transport.* J. Equine Sci. 7: 21-26.

Leadon, D.P. (1989) *A preliminary report on studies on equine transit stress.* J. Equine Vet. Sci. 9: 200-202.

Leadon, D.P., Frank, J., Backhouse, W., Frank, C. and Atock, M.A. (1990) *Environmental, haematological and blood biochemical changes in equine transit stress.* In: Proc. 36th Ann. Conf. AAEP 36: 485-490.

Leadon, D.P. (1994) *Transport stress.* In: Hodgson, D.R. and Rose, R.J., eds., The Athletic Horse, W.B.Saunders, Philadelphia, pp. 371-378.

Mair, T.S. and Lane, J.G. (1989) *Pneumonia, lung abscesses and pleuritis in adult horses: a review of 51 cases.* Equine vet. J. 21: 175-180.

McCarthy, R., Jeffcott, L. Clarke, I., Funder, J., Smith, I. and Wallace, C.A. (1991) *Evaluation of stress in horses.* Aust. Equine Vet. 9:34.

McClintock, S.A. and Begg, A.P. (1990) *Suspected salmonellosis in seven broodmares after transportation.* Aust. Vet. J. 67: 265-267.

Mills, P.C. and Marlin, D.J. (1996) *Plasma iron in elite horses at rest and after transport.* Vet. Rec. 139: 215-217.

Moberg, G. (1985) *Animal Stress.* American Physiological Society, Baltimore, MD.

* Momoi, Y., Kato, H., Youn, H.-Y., Aida, H., Takagi, S., Watari, T., Goitsuka, R., Tsujimoto, H. and Hasegawa, A. (1996) *Elevation of serum G-CSF level in horses with transportation-induced fever.* J. Vet. Med. Sci. 58: 537-541.

* Nambo, Y., Oikawa, M., Yoshihara, T., Kuwano, A., Hobo, S., Nagata, S., Watanabe, G. and Taya, K. (1996) *Effects of transport stress on concentrations of LH and FSH in plasma of mares: a preliminary study.* J. Equine Sci. 7: 1-5.

O'Callaghan, M.W., Hornof, W.J., Fisher, P.E. and Rabbe, O.G. (1987) *Ventilation imaging in the horse with ^{99m}technetium-DTPA radioaerosol.* Equine vet. J. 19: 19-24.

* Oikawa, M. and Kusunose, R. (1995) *Some epidemiological aspects of equine respiratory disease associated with transport.* J. Equine Sci. 6: 25-29.

* Oikawa, M., Kamada, M., Yoshikawa, Y. and Yoshikawa, T. (1994) *Pathology of equine pneumonia associated with transport and isolation of Streptococcus equi subsp. zooepidemicus.* J. Comp. Path. 111: 205-212.

* Oikawa, M., Takagi, S., Anzai, R., Yoshikawa, H. and Yoshikawa, T. (1995). *Pathology of equine respiratory disease occurring in association with transport.* J. Comp. Path. 113: 29-43.

Owen, R.A., Fullerton, J. and Barnum, D.A. (1983) *Effects of transportation, surgery, and antibiotic therapy in ponies infected with Salmonella.* Am. J. Vet. Res. 44: 46-50.

Perry, G. (1975) *Aspects of stress in man and animals.* Proc. Royal Soc. Med. 68: 423-425.

Racklyeft, D.J. and Love, D. (1990) *Influence of head posture on the respiratory tract of healthy horses.* Aust. Vet. J. 67: 402-405.

Raidal, S.L., Love, D.N. and Bailey, D.G. (1995) *Inflammation and increased numbers of bacteria in the lower respiratory tract of horses within 6 to 12 h of confinement with the head elevated.* Aust. Vet. J. 72: 45-50.

Raidal, S.L., Love, D.N. and Bailey, D.G. (1996) *Effects of posture and accumulated airway secretions on tracheal mucociliary transport in the horse.* Aust. Vet. J. 73: 45-49.

Raidal, S.L., Bailey, D.G. and Love, D.N. (1997) *Effect of transportation on lower respiratory tract contamination and peripheral blood neutrophil function.* Aust. Vet. J. 75: 433-438.

Raphel, C.F. and Beech, J. (1982) *Pleuritis secondary to pneumonia or lung abscessation in 90 horses.* JAVMA, 181: 808-810.

Rooney, J.R. (1991) *Pneumonia.* In: Beech, J., ed., Equine Respiratory Disorders, Lea and Febiger, Philadelphia, p. 149.

Schmidt, B. and Schmidt, K.H. (1980) *Effect of road transport, longeing, tournament and daytime on activities of serum enzymes aspartate aminotransferase, creatine kinase, lactate dehydrogenase, alkaline phosphatase and serum bilirubin in warm-blooded horses.* Berliner und Munchener Tierarztliche Wochenschrift 93: 244-246.

Selye, H. (1950) *Stress: the Physiology and Pathology of Exposure to Systematic Stress.* Acta, Inc., Montreal.

Sinha, S.K. and Abinanti, F.R. (1962) *Shipping fever of cattle.* Adv. Vet. Sci. Comp. Med. 17: 225-271.

Smith, B.L., Jones, J.H., Carlson, G.P. and Pascoe, J.R. (1994a) *Effect of body direction on heart rate in trailered horses.* Am. J. Vet. Res. 55: 1007-1011.

Smith, B.L., Jones, J.H., Carlson, G.P. and Pascoe, J.R. (1994b) *Body position and direction preferences in horses during road transport.* Equine vet. J. 26: 374-377.

Smith, B.L., Jones, J.H., Hornof, W.J., Miles, J.A., Longworth, K.E. and Willits, N.H. (1996a) *Effects of road transportation on indices of stress in horses.* Equine vet. J. 28: 446-454.

Smith, B.L., Miles, J.A., Jones, J.H. and Willits, N.H. (1996b) *Influence of suspension, tires, and shock absorbers on vibration in a two-horse trailer.* Trans. ASAE 39: 1083-1092.

Smith, B.L., Jones, J.H. and Miles, J.A. (1999) *Air flow patterns and ventilation in a two-horse trailer.* Trans. ASAE (in review).

Sonnichsen, H.V. and Jorgenssen, K. (1988) *Transport stress in horses.* Pferdeheilkunde 4: 35-36.

Stephens, D.B. (1980) *Stress and its measurement in domestic animals: a review of behavioral and physiolgical studies under field and laboratory conditions.* Adv. Vet. Sci. Comp. Med. 24: 179-210.

* Takagi, S. (1995) *Trial for prevention of equine pyrexia during transport.* Proc. World Vet. Congr. 33: 57.

Timoney, J. F., Anzai,T. and Blair, M. (1997) *Clonal invasion of the equine respiratory tract by Streptococcus zooepidemicus.* In: Horaud, T., ed., Streptococci and the Host, Plenum Press, New York, pp.611-633.

Traub-Dargatz, J.L., McKinnon, A.O., Bruyninckx, W.J., Thrall, M.A., Jones, R.L. and Blancquaert, A.M.N. (1988) *Effect of transportation stress on bronchoalveolar lavage fluid analysis in female horses.* Am. J. Vet. Res. 49:1026-1029.

van den Berg, J.S., Guthrie, A.J., Meintjes, R.A., Nurton, J.P., Adamson, D.A., Travers, C.W., Lund, R.J. and Mostert, H.J. (1998) *Water and electrolyte intake and output in conditioned Thoroughbred horses transported by road.* Equine vet. J. 30: 316-323.

Vogralik, M.V. and Poslov, G.A. (1981) *Biochemical basis of the reaction of racehorses to stressors.* Veterinariya Moscow USSR 4: 59-60.

Waran, N.K., Singh, N., Robertson, V., Cuddeford, D. and Marlin, D.J. (1993) *Effects of transport on behaviour and heart rates of Thoroughbred horses.* Appl. Anim. Behav. Sci. 38: 76.

Waran, N.K. (1993) *The behaviour of horses during and after transport by road.* Equine Vet. Educ. 5: 129-132.

Waran, N.K. and Cuddeford, D. (1995). *Effects of loading and transport on the heart rate and behaviour of horses.* Appl. Anim. Behav. Sci. 43: 71-81.

Waran, N.K., Robertson, V., Cuddeford, D., Kokoszko, A. and Marlin, D.J. (1996) *Effects of transporting horses facing either forwards or backwards on their behaviour and heart rate.* Vet. Rec. 139: 7-11.

Welsh, R.D. (1984) *The significance of Streptococcus zooepidemicus in the horse.* Equine Practice. 6: 6-26.

White, A., Reyes, A. Godoy, A. and Martinez, R. (1991) *Effects of transport and racing on ionic changes in Thoroughbred race horses.* Comp. Biochem. Physiol. 99A: 343-346.

Wi, L. and Chen, C.I. (1987) *Running and shipping elevate plasma level of beta-endorphin-like substance (B-END-LI) in Thoroughbred horses.* Life Sci. 40: 1411-1421.

* Yamauchi, T, Oikawa, M. and Hiraga, A. (1993) *Effects of transit stress on white blood cells count in the peripheral blood in Thoroughbred race horses.* Bull. Equine Res. Inst. 30: 30-32.

■ Body weight, rectal temperature, Haematology and blood biochemistry prior to transport and for three days after arrival, in racehorses transported by air to international races in Hong Kong

Leadon, D.P., Daykin, J. Backhouse, W. Frank, C. and Atock, A. (1990) *Environmental, haematological and blood biochemical changes in Equine Transit Stress.* Proc. A.A.E.P. Lexington, Kentucky, 485-490.

Rackyleft D.J. and Love D.N. (1990) *Influence of head posture on the respiratory tract health of horses.* Aust. Eq. Vet. 67.8 (3) 402.

Raidal, S.L., Taplin, R.H., Bailey, G.D. and Love, D.N. (1997) *Antibiotic prophylaxis of lower respiratory tract contamination in horses confined with head elevation for 24 or 48 hours.* Aust. Vet. J. 75, 126-131.

Schenker, M.B., Christiani, D., Cormier, Y., Dimich-Ward, H., Doekes, G., Dosman, J., Douwes, J., Dowling, K., Enarson, D., Green, F., Heederik, D., Husman, K., Kennedy, S., Kullman, G., Lacasse, Y., Lawson, B., Malmberg, P., May, J., McCurdy, S., Merchant, J., Myers, J., Nieuwenhuijsen, M., Olenchock, S., Saiki, C., Schwartz, D., Seiber, J., Thorne, P., Wagner, G., White, N., Xu, X. and Chan-Yeung, M. (1998) *Respiratory health hazards in agriculture.* Am. J. Resp. Crit. Care Med. 158, S1-S76.

Smith, B.L., Jones, J.H., Carlson, G.P. and Pascoe, J.R. (1994a) *Body position and direction preferences in horses during road transport.* Eq. Vet. J. 26, 374-377.

Smith, B.L., Jones, J.H., Carlson, G.P. and Pascoe, J.R. (1994b) *Effect of body direction on heart rate in trailered horses.* Am. J. Vet. Res. 55, 1007-1011.

Smith, B.L., Jones, J.H., Hornoff, W.J., Miles, J.A., Longworth, K.E. and Willits, N.H. (1996) *Effects of road transport on indices of stress in the horse.* Eq. Vet. J. 28, 446-454.

Traub-Dargatz, J.L., McKinnon, A.O., Bruyninkx, W.J., Thrall, M.A., Jones, R.L. and Blancquaert, A.M. (1988) *Effect of transportation stress on bronchoalveolar lavage fluid analysis in female horses.* Am. J. Vet. Res. 49, 1026-1029.

van den Berg, J.S., Guthrie, A.J., Meintjes, R.A., Nurton, J.P., Adamson, D.A., Travers, C.W., Lund, R.J. and Mostert H.J. (1998) *Water and electrolyte intake and output in conditioned Thoroughbred horses transported by road.* Eq. Vet. J. 30, 316-323.

Waran, N.K., Robertson, V. and Cuddefors, D. (1996) *Effects of transporting horses facing either forwards or backwards on their behaviour and heart rate.* Vet. Rec. 139, 7-11.

Woods, P.A., Robinson, N.E., Swanson, M.C., Reed, C.E., Broadstone, R.V. and Derksen, F.J. (1993) *Airborne dust and aeroallergen concentration in a horse stable under two different management systems.* Eq. Vet. J. 25, 208-213.

■ Effects of Transit on the Immune System of the Horse

Anderson, N.V., DeBowes, R.M., Nykop, K.A., Dayton, A.D. (1985) *Mononuclear phagocytes of transport-stressed horses with viral respiratory tract infection.* Am. J. Vet. Res. 46, 2272-2277.

Artursson, K., Wallgren, P., Alm, G.V. (1989) *Appearance of interferon-alpha in serum and signs of reduced immune function in pigs after transport and installation in a fattening farm.* Vet. Immunol. Immunopathol. 23, 345-353.

Austin, S.M., Foreman, J.H., Hungerford, L.L. (1995) *Case-control study of risk factors for development of pleuropneumonia in horses.* J. Am. Vet. Med. Assoc. 207, 325-328.

Baalsrud, K.J., Overnes, G. (1986) *Influence of vitamin E and selenium supplement on antibody production in horses.* Equine Vet. J. 18, 472-474.

Crisman, M.V., Hodgson, D.R., Bayly, W.M., Liggitt, H.D. (1992) *Effects of transport on constituents of bronchoalveolar lavage fluid from horses.* Cornell Vet. 82, 233-246.

Dalin, A.M., Magnusson, U., Haggendal, J., Nyberg, L. (1993) *The effect of transport stress on plasma levels of catecholamines, cortisol, corticosteroid-binding globulin, blood cell count, and lymphocyte proliferation in pigs.* Acta Vet. Scand. 34, 59-68.

Flaminio, M.J., Rush, B.R., Shuman, W. (1998) *Immunologic function in horses after non-specific immunostimulant administration.* Vet. Immunol. Immunopathol. 63, 303-315.

Gilmour, M.I., Park, P., Doerfler, D., Selgrade, M.K. (1993) *Factors that influence the suppression of pulmonary antibacterial defenses in mice exposed to ozone.* Exp. Lung Res. 19, 299-314.

Hobo, S., Oikawa, M., Kuwano, A., Yoshida, K., Yoshihara, T. (1997) *Effect of transportation on the composition of bronchoalveolar lavage fluid obtained from horses.* Am. J. Vet. Res. 58, 531-534.

Mackenzie, A.M., Drennan, M., Rowan, T.G., Dixon, J.B., Carter, S.D. (1997) *Effect of transportation and weaning on humoral immune responses of calves.* Res. Vet. Sci. 63, 227-30.

Moore, B.R. (1996) *Clinical application of interferons in large animal medicine.* J. Am. Vet. Med. Assoc. 208, 1711-1715.

Mudron, P., Kovac, G., Bajova, V., Pistl, J., Choma, J., Bartko, P., Scholz, H. (1994) *Effect of vitamin E on some leucocytic parameters and functions in transported calves.* DTW Dtsch. Tierarztl. Wochenschr. 101, 47-49.

Murata, H., Hirose, H. (1991) *Suppression of bovine lymphocyte and macrophage functions by sera from road-transported calves.* Br. Vet. J. 147, 455-462.

Murata, H., Miyamoto, T. (1993) *Bovine haptoglobin as a possible immunomodulator in the sera of transported calves.* Br. Vet. J. 149, 277-283.

Murata, H., Takahashi, H., Matsumoto, H. (1987) *The effects of road transportation on peripheral blood lymphocyte subpopulations, lymphocyte blastogenesis and neutrophil function in calves.* Br. Vet. J. 143, 166-174.

Oikawa, M., Jones, J.H. (1999) *Studies of the causes and effects of road transport stress in athletic horses.* Proceedings of the International Workshop on Equine Transport.

Raidal, S.L., Bailey, G.D., Love, D.N. (1997) *Effect of transportation on lower respiratory tract contamination and peripheral blood neutrophil function.* Aust. Vet. J. 75, 433-438.

Raidal, S.L., Love, D.N., Bailey, G.D. (1995) *Inflammation and increased numbers of bacteria in the lower respiratory tract of horses within 6 to 12 hours of confinement with the head elevated.* Aust. Vet. J. 72, 45-50.

Raidal, S.L., Taplin, R.H., Bailey, G.D., Love, D.N. (1997) *Antibiotic prophylaxis of lower respiratory tract contamination in horses confined with head elevation for 24 or 48 hours.* Aust. Vet. J. 75, 126-131.

Smith, B.L., Jones, J.H., Hornof, W.J., Miles, J.A., Longworth, K.E., Willits, N.H. (1996) *Effects of road transport on indices of stress in horses.* Equine Vet. J. 28, 446-454.

Traub-Dargatz, J.L., McKinnon, A.O., Bruyninckx, W.J., Thrall, M.A., Jones, R.L., Blancquaert, A.M. (1998) *Effect of transportation stress on bronchoalveolar lavage fluid analysis in female horses.* Am. J. Vet. Res. 49, 1096-1099.

■ Does Transport Stress affect Exercise Performance in Horses?

Arendt, J., Aldhous, M. and English, J. (1987) *The effects of jet-lag and their alleviation by melatonin.* Ergonomics 30, 1379-1393.

Atkinson, G. (1994) *Effects of age on human circadian rhythms in physiological and performance measures*, PhD Dissertation, John Moores University, Liverpool.

Atkinson, G., Coldwells, A. and Reilly, T. (1993) *Circadian rhythmicity in self-chosen work-rate. In: Chronobiology and chronomedicine*, Eds: C. Gutenbrunner, G. Hildebrandt, and R. Moog, Peter Lang-Verlag, Frankfurt, pp 478-484.

Atkinson, G., Greeves, J. and Cable, T. (1995) *Day-to-day and circadian variability of leg strength measured with the LIDO isokinetic dynamometer.* J. Sports Sci. 13, 18-19.

Atkinson, G. and Reilly, T. (1996) *Circadian variation in sports performance.* Sports Med. 21, 292-312.

Atkinson, G., Reilly, T. and Waterhouse, J. (1997) *Pharmacology and the travelling athlete.* In: A clinical pharmacology of sports and exercise, Eds: T. Reilly and M. Orme, Elsevier, Amsterdam, pp 293-301.

Beaunoyer, D.E. and Chapman, J.D. (1987) *The effects of trailering stress on subsequent submaximal exercise performance.* Proc. Eq. Nutr. Physiol. Soc., 379-384.

Boulos, Z., Campbell, S.C. and Strogatz, S.H. (1995) *Light treatment for sleep disorders: consensus report VII.* Jet lag. J. Biol. Rhythms 10, 167-176.

Codazza, D., Genchi, C., Agnes, F. and Matteo, G. (1974) *Serum enzyme changes and haematolo-chemical levels in thoroughbreds after transport and exercise.* J. So. Afr. Vet. Assn. 45, 331-334.

Cole, R.J. and Kripke, D.F. (1989) *Amelioration of jet lag by bright light treatment: effects on sleep consolidation.* Sleep Res. 18, 411.

Dawson, D. and Encel, N. (1993) Melatonin and sleep in humans. J. Pineal Res. 15, 1-12.

Doherty, O., Booth, M., Waran, N., Salthouse, C. and Cuddeford, D. (1997) *Study of the heart rate and energy expenditure of ponies during transport.* Vet. Rec. 141, 589-592.

Evans, J.W., Winget, C.M., DeRoshia, C. and Holley, D.C. (1978) *Ovulation and equine body temperature and heart rate circadian rhythms.* Journal of Interdisciplinary Cycle Research 7, 25-37.

Friend, T.H., Martin, M.T., Householder, D.D. and Bushong, D.M. (1998) *Stress responses of horses during a long period of transport in a commercial truck.* J. Amer. Vet. Med. Assoc. 212, 838-844.

Gifford, L.S. (1987) *Circadian variation in human flexibility.* Austr. J. Physiother. 33, 3-9.

Graeber, R.C. (1982) *Alterations in performance following rapid transmeridian flight.* In: Rhythmic aspects of behavior, Eds: F. M. Brown and R. C. Graeber, Erlbaum Associates, Hillsdale, NJ, pp 173-212.

Hauty, G.T. and Adams, T. (1966) *Phase shifts of the human circadian system and performance deficits during periods of transition.* Aerospace Med. 37, 1027-1033.

Hill, D.W. and Darnaby, K.M. (1992) *Effect of time of day on aerobic and anaerobic responses to high intensity exercise.* Can. J. Sports Sci. 17, 316-319.

Houpt, K.A. (1980) Equine behavior. Equine Practice 2, 8-12.

Irvine, and Alexander. (1994) *Factors affecting the circadian rhythm in plasma cortisol concentrations in the horse.* Dom. Anim. Endocrinol. 11, 227-238.

Japanese Equine Research Institute. (1977) *Effect of road transportation between Miho Training Center and Tokyo Race Track on athletic performance in racehorses.* Juui Gijutsu 15, 501-565 (written in Japanese).

Jehue, R., Street, D. and Huizenga, R. (1993) *Effect of time zone change and game time changes on team performance: National Football League.* Med. Sci. Sports Exercise 25, 127-131.

Kaseda, Y. and Ogawa, H. (1992) *Dirunal and seasonal rhythms in heart rate, body temperature, and daily activity of Misaki feral horses.* Jap. J. Equine Sci. 3, 1163-171.

Klein, K.E. and Wegmann, H. (1974) *The resynchronization of human circadian rhythms after transmeridian flights as a result of flight direction and mode of activity.* In: Chronobiology, Eds: L. D. Scheving, F. Halberg, and J. Pauly, Igaku-Shoin, Tokyo, pp 564-570.

Klein, K.E., Wegmann, H.M. and Hunt, B.I. (1972) *Desynchronization of body temperature and performance circadian rhythm as a result of outgoing and homegoing transmeridian flights.* Aerospace Med. 43, 119-132.

Kleitman, N. (1963) *Sleep and wakefulness*, University of Chicago Press, Chicago.

Krauchi, K., Cajochen, C. and Mori, D. (1997) *Early evening melatonin and S-20098 advance circadian phase and nocturnal regulation of core body termperature.* Am. J. Physiol. 41, R1178-R1188.

Lavie, P., Haimov, I. and Shochat, T. (1997) *Melatonin: shutting off the wakefulness system.* Front. Hormone Res. 23, 149-160.

Lewy, A., Wehr, T. and Goodwin, G. (1980) *Light suppresses melatonin secretion in humans.* Science 210, 1267-1269.

Luna, S.P.L. (1993) *Equine opiod, endocrine and metabolic responses to anaesthesia, exercise, transport and acupuncture*, PhD, University of Cambridge, Cambridge.

Manfredini, R., Manfredini, F., Fersini, C. and Conconi, F. (1998) *Circadian rhythms, athletic performance, and jet lag.* Brit. J. Sports Med. 32, 101-106.

Mars, L.A., Kiesling, H.A., Ross, T.T., Armstrong, J.B. and Murray, L. (1992) *Water acceptance and intake in horses under shipping stress.* Equine vet. J. 12, 17-20.

McNair, D.M., Lorr, M. and Droppleman, L.F. (1971) *EITS manual for the profile of mood states.*, Educational and Industrial Testing Service, San Diego.

Mejean, L., Kolopp, M. and Drouin, P. (1992) *Chronobiology, nutrition, and diabetes mellitus.* In: Biological rhythms in clinical and laboratory medicine, Eds: Y. Touitou and E. Haus, Springer-Verlag, Berlin, pp 375-385.

Monk, T.H. (1992) *Chronobiology of mental performance.* In: Biological rhythms in clinical and laboratory medicine, Eds: Y. Touitou and E. Hause, Springer-Verlag, Berlin, pp 208-213.

O'Connor, P.J. and Morgan, W.P. (1990) *Athletic performance following rapid traversal of multiple time zones.* Journal of Sports Medicine 10, 20-30.

O'Connor, P.J., Morgan, W.P., Koltyn, K.F., Raglin, J.S., Turner, J.G. and Kalin, N.H. (1991) *Air travel across four time zones in college swimmers.* J. appl. Physiol. 70, 756-763.

Recht, L.D., Lew, R.A. and Schwartz, W.J. (1995) *Baseball teams beaten by jet lag.* Nature 377, 583.

Reilly, T., Atkinson, G. and Waterhouse, J. (1997) *Travel fatigue and jet-lag.* Journal of Sports Sciences 15, 365-369.

Sasaki, M., Kurosaki, Y. and Onda, M. (1989) *Effects of bright light on circadian rhythmicity and sleep after transmeridian flight.* Sleep Res. 18, 442.

Shephard, R.J. (1984) *Sleep, biorhythms, and human performance.* Sports Med. 1, 11-37.

Smith, B.L., Jones, J. H., Carlson, G. P. and Pascoe, J. R. (1994) *Effect of body direction on heart rate in trailered horses.* Am. J. Vet. Res. 55, 1007-1011.

Smith, B.L., Jones, J.H., Hornof, W.J., Miles, J.A., Longworth, K.E. and Willits, N.H. (1996) *Effects of road transport on indices of stress in horses.* Equine vet. J. 28, 446-454.

Steenland, K. and Deddens, J.A. (1997) *Effect of travel and rest on performance of professional basketball players.* Sleep 20, 366-369.

Suvanto, S. and Harma, M. (1993) *The prediction of the adaptation of circadian rhythms to rapid time zone changes.* Ergonomics 36, 111-116.

van den Berg, J.S., Guthrie, A.J., Meintjes, R.A., Nurton, J., Adamson, D., Travers, C. and Lund, R. (1998) *The effect of road transportation on external water and electrolyte balance of conditioned horses.* Equine vet. J. 30, 316-323.

Waran, N.K. (1997) *The physical effects of transport on competition horses.* J. equine vet. Sci. 17, 462.

Waterhouse, J., Reilly, T. and Atkinson, G. (1998) *Melatonin and jet lag.* Journal of Sports Medicine 32, 98-99.

Winget, C.M., DeRoshia, C.W. and Holley, D.C. (1985) *Circadian rhythms and athletic performance.* Med. Sci. Sports Exercise 17, 498-516.

Winget, C.M., Deroshia, C.W., Markley, C.L. and Holley, D.C. (1984) *A review of human physiological and performance changes associated with desynchronosis of biological rhythms.* Aviat. Space Environ. Med. 55, 1085-1096.

Wright, W.E., Vogel, J.A., Sampson, J.B., Knapik, J.J., Patton, J.F. and Daniels, W.L. (1983) *Effects of travel across time zones (jet-lag) on exercise capacity and performance.* Aviat. Space Environ. Med. 54, 132-137.